Animal Health Act 1981

CHAPTER 22

ARRANGEMENT OF SECTIONS

PART I

GENERAL

A

ELIZABETH II

Animal Health Act 1981

1981 CHAPTER 22

An Act to consolidate the Diseases of Animals Act 1935,
the Diseases of Animals Act 1950, the Ponies Act 1969,
the Rabies Act 1974, the Diseases of Animals Act 1975,
and certain related enactments.   [11th June 1981]

B E IT ENACTED by the Queen's most Excellent Majesty, by and
with the advice and consent of the Lords Spiritual and
Temporal, and Commons, in this present Parliament
assembled, and by the authority of the same, as follows:—

PART I

GENERAL

*General powers of Ministers to make orders and
to authorise regulations*

1. The Ministers may make such orders as they think fit— General

    (*a*) generally for the better execution of this Act, or for the powers of
purpose of in any manner preventing the spreading of Ministers to
disease ; and make orders.

    (*b*) in particular for the several purposes set out in this
Act, and for prescribing and regulating the payment
and recovery of expenses in respect of animals.

2. The Ministers may make such orders as they think fit for Local
authorising a local authority to make regulations for any of the authority
purposes— regulations.

    (*a*) of this Act, or

    (*b*) of an order of the Minister,

A 3

subject to such conditions, if any, as the Ministers for the purpose of securing uniformity and the due execution of this Act, think fit to prescribe.

Eradication and prevention of disease

Expenditure for eradication.

3.—(1) The Ministers may, with the Treasury's approval, expend such sums as they think fit with the object of eradicating as far as practicable diseases of animals (including horses) in Great Britain.

In this subsection " disease " is not restricted by its definition in this Act.

(2) To obtain information required for the purposes of subsection (1) above the Ministers may authorise in writing any veterinary inspector or other officer of the Ministry to inspect animals (including horses).

(3) A person so authorised may, for the purpose of any inspection to be carried out by him—

(a) at all reasonable times, and

(b) upon production of his authority on demand,

enter on any land or premises and apply such tests and take such samples as he considers necessary.

1950 c. 36.

(4) No payment may be made under subsection (1) which was capable of being made under section 3 of the Diseases of Animals Act 1950 (payments for the eradication of bovine tuberculosis) before the expiry of that section.

Offences as to s. 3.

4.—(1) A person who knowingly or recklessly makes any false statement for the purpose of obtaining for himself or any other person any sum payable under section 3 above shall (unless in the case of an indictable offence he is indicted for the offence) be liable on summary conviction—

(a) to a fine not exceeding £100 ; or

(b) to imprisonment for a term not exceeding 3 months ; or

(c) to both such imprisonment and fine.

(2) A person who obstructs or impedes any person duly authorised under subsection (2) of section 3 to make any inspection shall be liable on summary conviction—

(a) in the case of a first offence, to a fine not exceeding £50 ; and

(b) in the case of a second or subsequent offence punishable under this subsection—

(i) to a fine not exceeding £50 ; or

(ii) to imprisonment for a term not exceeding one month ; or

(iii) to both such imprisonment and fine.

In considering for the purposes of this subsection or subsection (2) of section 30 of the Agriculture Act 1937 whether an offence is or is not a first offence, references to an offence punishable under this subsection or that subsection shall be taken as including references to offences punishable under that subsection or this subsection, as the case may be.

1937 c. 70

5.—(1) Without prejudice to the generality of section 3 above, the Ministers have power, with the Treasury's approval, to afford veterinary services, including diagnostic services, whether free of charge or not, to persons—

Veterinary services and therapeutic substances.

(*a*) who carry on livestock businesses ; and

(*b*) who participate in arrangements approved by the Ministers as being satisfactory arrangements for keeping their stock so far as practicable free from disease and in good health.

In this subsection " disease " is not restricted by its definition in this Act.

(2) Schedule 1 to this Act has effect in relation to the regulation of the manufacture of and other matters connected with veterinary therapeutic substances.

6. The Ministers may make orders—

Eradication areas and attested areas.

(*a*) declaring any area as respects which they are satisfied that a substantial majority of the cattle in that area are free from any particular disease to be an eradication area for purposes connected with the control of that disease ;

(*b*) declaring any area as respects which they are satisfied that any particular disease of cattle is for practical purposes non-existent in that area to be an attested area for purposes connected with the control of that disease ; and

(*c*) prohibiting or regulating the movement of cattle into, out of or within any area which is for the time being an eradication area or an attested area or, if the area is an eradication area or an attested area for purposes connected with the control of brucellosis, imposing with respect to cattle in that area such other prohibitions or requirements as they may consider necessary or desirable for the purpose of eradicating that disease.

Cleansing and disinfection.

7.—(1) The Ministers may make such orders as they think fit—

> (*a*) for prescribing and regulating the cleansing and disin-
> fection of places used for the holding of markets, fairs,
> exhibitions, or sales of animals, or for lairage of
> animals, and yards, sheds, stables, and other places
> used for animals ;
>
> (*b*) for prescribing and regulating the cleansing and disin-
> fection of vessels, aircraft, vehicles, and pens and other
> places, used for the carrying of animals for hire or con-
> nected purposes ;
>
> (*c*) for prescribing and regulating the disinfection of the
> clothes of persons coming in contact with or employed
> about diseased or suspected animals and the use of
> precautions against the spreading of disease by such
> persons ;
>
> (*d*) for prescribing modes of cleansing and disinfection.

(2) The Ministers may by orders prescribe and regulate the cleansing and disinfection of receptacles or vehicles used for the conveyance or exposure for sale of poultry.

Movement generally.

8.—(1) The Ministers may make such orders as they think fit—

> (*a*) for prescribing and regulating the marking of animals ;
>
> (*b*) for prohibiting or regulating the movement of animals,
> and the removal of carcases, fodder, litter, dung
> and other things, and for prescribing and regulating
> the isolation of animals newly purchased ;
>
> (*c*) for prescribing and regulating the issue and production
> of licences respecting movement and removal of
> animals and things ;
>
> (*d*) for prohibiting, absolutely or conditionally, the use, for
> the carrying of animals or for any connected purpose,
> of a vessel, aircraft, vehicle, or pen or other place in
> respect of which or the use of which a penalty has been
> recovered from any person for an offence against this
> Act ;
>
> (*e*) for prohibiting or regulating the holding of markets, fairs,
> exhibitions and sales of animals.

(2) A person is guilty of an offence against this Act if, where an order of the Minister absolutely or conditionally prohibits the use of a vessel, aircraft, vehicle or pen, or other place, for the carrying of animals or for any connected purpose, he, without lawful authority or excuse, proof of which shall lie on him, does anything so prohibited.

Transport by sea and air

9. The Ministers may make such orders as they think fit for prohibiting the conveyance of animals by any specified vessel or aircraft to or from any port or aerodrome in the United Kingdom for such time as the Ministers may consider expedient.

10.—(1) The Ministers may by orders make such provision as they think fit for the purpose of preventing the introduction or spreading of disease into or within Great Britain through the importation of—

(*a*) animals and carcases ;

(*b*) carcases of poultry and eggs ; and

(*c*) other things, whether animate or inanimate, by or by means of which it appears to them that any disease might be carried or transmitted.

(2) Without prejudice to the generality of the powers conferred by this section and by section 1 above, for the purpose specified in subsection (1) above an order under this section—

(*a*) may prohibit or regulate the importation of any of the things specified in paragraphs (*a*) to (*c*) of subsection (1) ;

(*b*) may make provision not only with respect to imports (including vessels, boats, aircraft and vehicles of other descriptions) but also with respect to persons, animals, and other things which have been or may have been in contact with imports ;

(*c*) may make different provision in relation to different cases ; and

(*d*) may make provision with respect to any of the matters specified in Schedule 2 to this Act.

(3) An order under this section may provide that, in such circumstances as may be specified in the order, animals which—

(*a*) are brought into Great Britain in such circumstances that they are not imported, within the meaning of this Act, and

(*b*) whilst outside Great Britain have been or may have been in contact with any of the things specified in paragraphs (*a*) to (*c*) of subsection (1),

shall be deemed for the purposes of this section and Schedule 2 to be imported at the time when they are brought into Great Britain.

(4) In this section and in Schedule 2 " animals " includes—

(*a*) any kind of mammal, except man,

(*b*) any kind of four-footed beast which is not a mammal, and

(c) fish, reptiles, crustaceans and other cold-blooded crea-
              tures not falling within paragraph (a) or paragraph (b)
              above,
and " disease " is not restricted by its definition in this Act.

(5) An order under this section which is expressed to be made
for the purpose of preventing the introduction of rabies into
Great Britain may include provision for the destruction, by
such persons as may be prescribed by the order, of animals in
respect of which the order or any licence granted under it is
contravened.

(6) Every order made under this section shall be laid before
both Houses of Parliament after being made.

(7) Paragraphs (a) and (b) of section 5(2) of the Customs and
Excise Management Act 1979 (time of importation of goods
brought by sea and air) have effect for the purposes of this section
and Schedule 2 as they have effect for the purposes of the customs
and excise Acts.

(8) The landing of imported animals in Great Britain shall be
effected in such manner, at such times and subject to such super-
vision as the Commissioners of Customs and Excise may direct.

Export to   **11.** The Minister may by order make provision in the interests
member States. of animal health or of human health, for regulating the exportation from Great Britain to a member State of animals or
animal or poultry carcases, and in particular—

          (a) for prohibiting exportation without such certificate or
              licence as may be prescribed by the order, and

          (b) as to the circumstances in which and conditions on
              which a certificate or licence may be obtained.

Export   **12.**—(1) For the purpose of preventing the conveyance of
quarantine   disease by animals exported from Great Britain, the appropriate
stations.   Minister, with the Treasury's consent, may—

          (a) provide facilities for the examination of animals intended
              for export ; and

          (b) provide or approve one or more quarantine stations for
              the reception, isolation and examination of such
              animals.

A quarantine station so provided or approved is in this Act
referred to as an " export quarantine station ".

(2) Notwithstanding anything in this Act, compensation shall not be payable under this Act in respect of any animal intended for export, which by reason of—

(*a*) its having been diseased or suspected, or

(*b*) its having been exposed to the infection of any disease, is slaughtered in an export quarantine station.

Control of dogs, and preventive treatment of sheep

13.—(1) The Minister may make such orders as he thinks fit Orders as to for prescribing and regulating— dogs.

(*a*) the muzzling of dogs, and the keeping of dogs under control ; and

(*b*) so far as is supplemental to paragraph (*a*) above—

(i) the seizure, detention, and disposal (including slaughter) of stray dogs and of dogs not muzzled, and of dogs not being kept under control ; and

(ii) the recovery from the owners of dogs of the expenses incurred in respect of their detention.

(2) The appropriate Minister may make such orders as he thinks fit—

(*a*) for prescribing and regulating the wearing by dogs, while in a highway or in a place of public resort, of a collar with the name and address of the owner inscribed on the collar or on a plate or a badge attached to it ;

(*b*) with a view to the prevention of worrying of animals (including horses), for preventing dogs or any class of dogs from straying during all or any of the hours between sunset and sunrise ;

(*c*) for providing that any dog in respect of which an offence is being committed against provisions made under either paragraph (*a*) or (*b*) above, may be seized and treated as a stray dog under the enactments relating to dogs ;

(*d*) for prescribing and regulating—

(i) the seizure, detention and disposal (including slaughter) of stray dogs and of dogs not muzzled ; and

(ii) the recovery from the owners of dogs of the expenses incurred in respect of their detention.

14.—(1) The Ministers may make such orders as they think fit Prevention of for prescribing, regulating and securing the periodical treatment sheep scab. of all sheep by effective dipping or by the use of some other remedy for sheep scab.

(2) An inspector of the Minister and, if so authorised by order of the Minister, an inspector of the local authority, may—

    (*a*) subject to the directions of the authority by which he was appointed, and

    (*b*) for the purposes of any order or regulation under sub-section (1) above,

enter any premises and examine any sheep on those premises.

(3) The owner and the person in charge of any sheep shall comply with all reasonable requirements of the inspector as to the collection and penning of the sheep and afford all other reasonable facilities for the examination of the sheep by the inspector.

PART II

DISEASE

Outbreak

Separation and notice.

15.—(1) Any person having in his possession or under his charge an animal affected with disease shall—

    (*a*) as far as practicable keep that animal separate from animals not so affected ; and

    (*b*) with all practicable speed give notice of the fact of the animal being so affected to a constable of the police force for the police area in which the animal is so affected.

(2) Any person who knows or suspects that an animal (whether in captivity or not) is affected with rabies shall give notice of that fact to a constable unless—

    (*a*) he believes on reasonable grounds that another person has given notice under this section in respect of that animal, or

    (*b*) he is exempted from doing so by an order under section 1 above,

and, if the animal is in his possession or under his charge, shall as far as practicable keep the animal separate from other animals.

(3) The constable to whom notice is given shall forthwith give information of it to such person or authority as the Ministers by order direct.

(4) The Ministers may make such orders as they think fit for prescribing and regulating the notice to be given to or by any person or authority in case of any particular disease or in case of the illness of an animal, and for supplementing or varying for those purposes any of the provisions of subsections (1) to (3) above.

(5) Subsections (1) to (4) above do not have effect in relation to poultry, but the Ministers may by order prescribe and regulate—

    (*a*) the separation of diseased poultry from poultry not affected with disease ; and

    (*b*) the notification of disease in, or illness of, poultry.

(6) The local authority shall pay to a veterinary surgeon or veterinary practitioner, in respect of every notification of disease made by him to the local authority in pursuance of an order under this Act requiring such a notification, such fee not exceeding 12½p as may be prescribed by the order.

(7) A person is guilty of an offence against this Act who, without lawful authority or excuse, proof of which shall lie on him, fails where required by this Act or by an order of the Minister—

    (*a*) to keep an animal separate so far as practicable ; or

    (*b*) to give notice of disease with all practicable speed.

16.—(1) For the purpose of preventing the spread of disease, the Ministers may cause to be treated with serum or vaccine, or with both serum and vaccine, any animal or bird— Treatment after exposure to infection.

    (*a*) which has been in contact with a diseased animal or bird, or

    (*b*) which appears to the Ministers to be or to have been in any way exposed to the infection of disease ; or

    (*c*) which is in an infected area.

(2) The powers conferred by this section shall be construed as extending to the taking of any action—

    (*a*) which is requisite for enabling the appropriate treatment to be administered, or

    (*b*) which is otherwise required in connection with that treatment,

and for the purpose of exercising those powers any officer of the Minister may, subject to production of his authority on demand, enter any land or premises taking with him such other persons, if any, as he considers requisite.

Infection

17.—(1) The Ministers may make such orders as they think fit for prescribing the cases in which places and areas are to be declared to be infected with a disease and the authority, mode, and conditions by, in, and on which declarations in that behalf are to be made, and their effect and consequences, and their duration and discontinuance, and other connected matters. Powers as to infected places and areas.

(2) Every place or area so declared infected shall be an infected place or area for the purposes of this Act.

(3) A notice served in pursuance of directions of the Minister or of a local authority by virtue of an order made under this section shall be conclusive evidence to all intents of the existence or past existence or cessation of the disease, or of the error, and of any other matter on which the notice proceeds.

(4) Notwithstanding anything in this Act, a defined part of a port or aerodrome, or any part thereof, shall not be declared to be an infected place, or be made part of an infected place, otherwise than by the Ministers.

Other provisions as to infected places and areas.

18.—(1) Notwithstanding anything in this Act, where the Minister, on inquiry, and after communication with the local authority, is satisfied that a declaration of a place being an infected place has been made in error—

(a) respecting the existence or past existence of disease, or

(b) respecting the limits of a place, or

(c) respecting any other matter of fact on which the declaration proceeded,

the Minister may by order cancel the declaration as regards the infected place, or as regards any part of it, as he thinks fit.

(2) Where, in accordance with the provisions of this Act—

(a) a place or an area or a portion of an area is declared free from a disease, or

(b) a declaration of a place being an infected place is cancelled as regards the place or as regards any part of it,

then, from the time specified in that behalf by the Minister, or a local authority, as the case may be, the place, or area or that portion of the area or that part of the place, shall cease to be, or to be in, an infected place or area.

(3) An order of the Minister—

(a) declaring a place to be an infected place or area, or

(b) declaring a place or area, or a portion of an area, to be free from disease, or

(c) cancelling a declaration,

shall be conclusive evidence to all intents of the existence or past existence or cessation of the disease, or of the error, and of any other matter on which the order proceeds.

19.—(1) An order under section 17 above prescribing the cases in which areas are to be declared to be infected with rabies may include provision for the destruction in an area declared to be so infected, by persons authorised in accordance with the order, of foxes and such other wild mammals as may be prescribed by the order (not in either case being animals held in captivity). PART II
Destruction of foxes etc. on rabies infection.

(2) An order made by virtue of subsection (1) above may provide for—

(a) authorising any person to enter any land (other than a dwellinghouse) for the purpose of carrying out, or of deciding whether to carry out, the destruction there of animals in accordance with the order ;

(b) authorising the erection of fences or other obstacles to restrict the movement of animals into and out of an area where destruction is carried out ;

(c) regulating the ownership and disposal of the carcases of animals destroyed in accordance with the order ;

(d) prohibiting any person from obstructing the destruction of animals in accordance with the order and from interfering with the carcases of animals destroyed ;

(e) authorising the use of methods of destruction which would otherwise be unlawful.

(3) An order made by virtue of subsection (1) shall include provision as to the steps to be taken to inform the occupier of any land where it is proposed that animals should be destroyed, and other persons who may be there, of the proposal and of the methods of destruction to be used.

20.—(1) An order under section 17 above prescribing the cases in which areas are to be declared to be infected with rabies may include provision for— Additional provisions under s. 17 on rabies infection.

(a) requiring notice to be given, in such circumstances as may be prescribed by the order, of the death in an area declared to be so infected of such domestic or wild mammals as may be prescribed ;

(b) regulating the ownership and disposal of the carcases of animals whose deaths are required to be notified by virtue of paragraph (a) above ;

(c) requiring and regulating the vaccination, confinement and control in such area of such domestic mammals and mammals held in captivity as may be prescribed by the order ;

(*d*) authorising the seizure and detention and the disposal or destruction of any animal in respect of which any provision made by virtue of paragraph (*c*) above is not complied with ;

(*e*) authorising any person to enter any land for the purpose of seizing or destroying any animal in pursuance of the order.

(2) An order under section 17 prescribing the cases in which areas are to be declared to be infected with rabies may provide—

(*a*) for the division of an area into zones (whether defined by reference to distance from the places within the area where diseased animals have been found or otherwise) ; and

(*b*) for the consequences which may follow a declaration to be different for different zones.

Destruction of
wild life on
infection other
than rabies.

21.—(1) This section—

(*a*) applies to any disease other than rabies which is for the time being a disease for the purposes of section 1(*a*) above ; and

(*b*) is without prejudice to any powers conferred by other provisions of this Act on the Minister, the appropriate Minister and the Ministers.

(2) The Minister, if satisfied in the case of any area—

(*a*) that there exists among the wild members of one or more species in the area a disease to which this section applies which has been or is being transmitted from members of that or those species to animals of any kind in the area, and

(*b*) that destruction of wild members of that or those species in that area is necessary in order to eliminate, or substantially reduce the incidence of, that disease in animals of any kind in the area,

may, subject to the following provisions of this section, by order provide for the destruction of wild members of that or those species in that area.

(3) Before making an order under this section the Minister shall consult with the Nature Conservancy Council, and every order so made shall specify—

(*a*) the area to which it applies ;

(*b*) the disease to which it applies ; and

(*c*) the one or more species to which it relates.

(4) An order under this section providing for the destruction of wild members of one or more species in any area may provide for authorising the use for that purpose of one or more methods of destruction that would otherwise be unlawful.

The order shall not authorise such use unless the Minister is satisfied that use of the method or methods in question is the most appropriate way of carrying out that destruction, having regard to all relevant considerations and, in particular, the need to avoid causing unnecessary suffering to wild members of the species in question.

(5) An order under this section may include provision—

   (*a*) for ensuring that destruction of wild members of any species to which the order relates is properly and effectively carried out, and in particular—

      (i) for preventing persons from taking into captivity harbouring, concealing or otherwise protecting wild members of any such species with intent to prevent their destruction, or

      (ii) in any other way obstructing or interfering with anything which has been, is being or is to be done or used in connection with that destruction ·

   (*b*) for regulating the ownership and disposal of the carcases of members of any such species destroyed in the area to which the order relates.

(6) Before commencing the destruction of wild members of a species on any land within an area to which an order under this section applies the Minister shall take all reasonable steps to inform—

   (*a*) the occupier of the land, and

   (*b*) any other person who may be there,

of his intention to carry out that destruction and of the methods of destruction to be used.

It shall be the Minister's duty to ensure that destruction is carried out on any such land in as safe a manner as is possible in all the circumstances.

(7) Where an order under this section is in force, the Minister shall have power to take such measures (including the erection of fences or other obstacles) as he considers appropriate—

   (*a*) for preventing the movement of living creatures into or out of the area or any part of the area to which the order applies while destruction of wild members of any species to which the order relates is being carried out in the area ; and (*b*) where destruction of wild members of any such species has been or is to be carried out in any part of that area, for preventing the recolonisation of that part by members of that species for as long as he considers necessary to prevent reappearance among them of the disease to which the order applies.

(8) As soon as may be after the Minister is satisfied, in the case of any land, that any measures affecting that land which have been taken in connection with an order under this section are no longer necessary, he shall—

    (*a*) remove from the land anything placed or erected on it ; and

    (*b*) take such other steps as are reasonably practicable to reinstate the land.

(9) In this section and section 22 below—

" animals " includes horses,

" species " means any species of bird or mammal, except man,

and references to wild members of any species in an area are references to members of the species in the area that are neither domesticated nor held in captivity.

(10) A statutory instrument containing an order under this section shall be subject to annulment in pursuance of a resolution of either House of Parliament.

Powers of
entry etc. for
s. 21.

22.—(1) In relation to any disease to which section 21 above applies the following persons are authorised officers for the purposes of this section—

    (*a*) an officer of the appropriate Minister,

    (*b*) a veterinary inspector, and

    (*c*) any person who, not being such an officer or inspector, is authorised by the appropriate Minister to exercise the powers conferred by this section,

and subsection (9) of section 21 applies to this section.

(2) Where an authorised officer has reasonable grounds for suspecting, in the case of any area, that there exists among the wild members of any species in the area a disease to which section 21 applies, he may enter any land in the area and—

    (*a*) take samples of the wild members of that species, or of their excreta, or of any materials (whether or not forming part of the land) with which wild members of that species may have been in contact ;

(*b*) carry out any other investigations which he considers necessary for the purpose of determining, as regards that species and that disease, whether an order under section 21 should be made in respect of the whole or part of the area in question.

(3) An authorised officer may at any time enter any land in the area to which an order under section 21 applies for any of the following purposes—

(*a*) to carry out the destruction of any wild members of a species to which the order relates that may be on that land ;

(*b*) to take any such measures as are mentioned in subsection (7) of that section ;

(*c*) to ascertain, as regards any wild members of a species to which the order relates, whether destruction has been effectively carried out.

(4) Where in pursuance of an order under section 21 destruction of wild members of any species to which the order relates has been carried out on any land in the area to which the order applies, then, for the purpose of ascertaining—

(*a*) whether the land has been or is being recolonised by wild members of that species, and, if so,

(*b*) whether there exists among them the disease to which the order applies (or, if the order has been revoked, to which it previously applied),

an authorised officer may enter the land and take such samples of or relating to that species as are mentioned in paragraph (*a*) of subsection (2) above ; but the powers conferred by this subsection shall not be exercisable at any time more than 2 years after the revocation of the order in question.

(5) Nothing in this section authorises any person to enter a dwellinghouse.

(6) A person entering any land in the exercise of powers conferred on him by this section shall, if so required by the owner or occupier or person in charge of the land—

(*a*) produce to him some duly authenticated document showing his authority ; and

(*b*) state in writing his reasons for entering.

(7) Without prejudice to subsection (6) above, an authorised officer—

(*a*) shall not demand admission as of right to any land forming part of a nature reserve (within the meaning of section 15 of the National Parks and Access to the Countryside Act 1949) maintained or managed by the 1949 c. 97

A 6

Nature Conservancy Council under section 1 of the Nature Conservancy Council Act 1973 unless 7 days' notice of the intended entry has been given to the Council ; and

(b) in exercising any of his powers under subsection (2), (3) or (4) above on any such land shall, as far as possible, do so in accordance with such reasonable requirements for minimising damage to flora, fauna or geological or physiographical features within the reserve as may have been notified by the Council to the appropriate Minister.

(8) The preceding provisions of this section are without prejudice to any powers conferred on inspectors or others by or by virtue of any other provision of this Act.

Orders as to infected places and areas.

23. The Ministers may make such orders as they think fit for all or any of the following purposes—

(a) for prescribing and regulating the publication by placards, handbills, or otherwise, in the immediate neighbourhood of a place or area declared infected, of the fact of such declaration ;

(b) for prohibiting or regulating the movement of animals and persons into, within, or out of an infected place or area ;

(c) for prescribing and regulating the isolation or separation of animals being in an infected place or area ;

(d) for prohibiting or regulating the removal of carcases, fodder, litter, utensils, pens, hurdles, dung, or other things into, within, or out of an infected place or area ;

(e) for prescribing and regulating the destruction, burial, disposal, or treatment of carcases, fodder, litter, utensils, pens, hurdles, dung, or other things, being in or removed from an infected place or area ;

(f) for prescribing and regulating the cleansing and disinfection of infected places and areas, or parts of them ;

(g) for prescribing and regulating the disinfection of the clothes of persons being in an infected place, and the use of precautions against the spreading of disease by such persons.

Rabies: quarantine and virus control.

24. The provision which may be made by orders under section 1 above shall (without prejudice to the generality of that provision) include provision—

(a) for requiring mammals which may be carriers of rabies to be kept in quarantine in such cases, for such periods and under such conditions as may be prescribed by the order ;

(*b*) for prohibiting or regulating—

      (i) the keeping and importation of rabies virus in any form ; and

      (ii) the deliberate introduction of the virus into animals.

25. The Ministers may make such orders as they think fit for all or any of the following purposes— Movement of
diseased or
suspected
animals.

    (*a*) for prohibiting or regulating the exposure of diseased or suspected animals in markets or fairs or sale-yards, or other public or private places, where animals are commonly exposed for sale, and their placing in lairs or other places adjacent to or connected with markets or fairs, or where animals are commonly placed before exposure for sale ;

    (*b*) for prohibiting or regulating the sending or carrying of diseased or suspected animals, or of dung or other thing likely to spread disease, or causing them to be sent or carried, on railways, canals, rivers, or inland navigations, or in coasting vessels, or in an aircraft engaged in a flight or a part of a flight beginning and ending in Great Britain, or otherwise ;

    (*c*) for prohibiting or regulating the carrying, leading, or driving of diseased or suspected animals, or causing them to be carried, led or driven, on highways or thoroughfares, or elsewhere ;

    (*d*) for prohibiting or regulating the placing or keeping of diseased or suspected animals on commons or unenclosed lands, or in fields or other places insufficiently fenced, or on the sides of highways.

26.—(1) The Minister shall by orders make such provision as he thinks necessary or expedient respecting the case of animals found to be affected with pleuro-pneumonia or foot-and-mouth disease— Pleuro-
pneumonia or
foot-and-
mouth disease
found in
transit.

    (*a*) while exposed for sale or exhibited in a market, fair, sale-yard, place of exhibition, or other place ; or

    (*b*) while placed in a lair or other place before exposure for sale ; or

    (*c*) while in transit or in course of being moved by land, water or air ; or

    (*d*) while being in a slaughter-house or place where animals are slaughtered or are kept with a view to slaughter ; or

    (*e*) while being on common or unenclosed land ; or

    (*f*) generally, while being in a place not in the possession or occupation or under the control of the owner of the animals.

(2) The Minister shall by orders under this section make such provision as he thinks fit for the consequences under this Act of animals being so found in the circumstances mentioned above—

(a) as well with regard to the animals as with regard to the places where they are when so found, and other places ; and

(b) with regard to animals being or having been in the same shed or stable, herd or flock as, or in contact with, animals so found.

(3) The Minister may, by orders under this section relating to particular places, make such provision as he thinks fit for the consequences mentioned above.

(4) Every order under this section shall have full effect not withstanding—

(a) any provision of this Act requiring the declaration of a place infected with pleuro-pneumonia or foot-and-mouth disease, or relating to any consequence of such a declaration, or to any matter connected with such a declaration ; and

(b) any other provision whatsoever of this Act.

Exclusion of strangers.

27.—(1) A person owning or having charge of any animals in a place or area declared infected with any disease may affix, at or near the entrance to a building or enclosure in which the animals are, a notice forbidding persons to enter the building or enclosure without the permission mentioned in the notice.

(2) Thereupon it shall not be lawful for any person, not having by law a right of entry or way into, on, or over that building or enclosure, to enter or go into, on, or over the building or enclosure without that permission.

Seizure of diseased or suspected animals.

28. The Ministers may make such orders as they think fit—

(a) for prescribing and regulating the seizure, detention and disposal of a diseased or suspected animal exposed, carried, kept or otherwise dealt with in contravention of an order of the Minister ; and

(b) for prescribing and regulating the liability of the owner or consignor or consignee of such animal to the expenses connected with its seizure, detention and disposal.

Risk to human health

Control of zoonoses.

29.—(1) This section shall have effect with a view to reducing the risk to human health from any disease of, or organism carried in, animals ; and the Ministers may by order designate any such disease or organism which in their opinion constitutes such a risk as is mentioned in this subsection.

In this section " disease " is not restricted by its definition in this Act.

(2) Where any disease or organism is for the time being designated under this section, the Ministers may by order—

(*a*) provide for any provision of this Act which has effect in relation to the disease to have that effect in relation to the disease so designated subject to such modifications as may be specified in the order ;

(*b*) apply any provision of this Act, subject to any modifications so specified, in relation to the presence of the organism in an animal as if the presence of the organism were a disease to which this Act applied.

(3) The Ministers may by order make provision for requiring a person who, in such circumstances as are specified by the order, knows or has reason to suspect that an animal of such description as is specified in the order is or was—

(*a*) affected with a disease designated under this section, or

(*b*) a carrier of an organism so designated,

to furnish to such person and in such form and within such period as are specified in the order such information relating to the animal as is so specified.

30.—(1) If it appears to the appropriate Minister that a person may have information relating to— Provisions supplemental to s. 29.

(*a*) an animal affected with a disease designated under section 29 above, or

(*b*) an animal which is a carrier of an organism so designated,

that Minister may by notice in writing require him to furnish to such person and in such form and within such period as are specified in the notice such information relating to the animal as he possesses and is so specified.

In this section " disease " is not restricted by its definition in this Act.

(2) Where a veterinary inspector has reason to believe that an animal such as is mentioned in subsection (1) above is or has been on any land he may, on producing if so required evidence of his authority—

(*a*) enter the land and make such tests and take such samples of any animal, feeding stuff, litter, dung, vessel, pen, vehicle or other thing whatsoever which is on or forms part of the land as he thinks appropriate for the purpose of ascertaining whether such an animal is or has been on the land ; and (*b*) require the owner or person having charge of any animals on the land to take such reasonable steps as the inspector may specify for the purpose of collecting or restraining them so as to facilitate the exercise in relation to them of the powers conferred on the inspector by paragraph (*a*) above.

(3) A person is guilty of an offence against this Act who—

(*a*) fails to comply with a requirement imposed on him by virtue of section 29 and this section ; or

(*b*) in purported compliance with a requirement to furnish information which is imposed on him by virtue of section 29 and this section, knowingly or recklessly furnishes information which is false in a material particular.

Slaughter

Slaughter in certain diseases.

31. Schedule 3 to this Act has effect as to the slaughter of animals in relation to—

(*a*) cattle plague ;

(*b*) pleuro-pneumonia ;

(*c*) foot-and-mouth disease ;

(*d*) swine-fever ; and

(*e*) diseases of poultry.

Slaughter in other diseases.

32.—(1) The Minister may, if he thinks fit, cause to be slaughtered any animal which—

(*a*) is affected or suspected of being affected with any disease to which this section applies ; or

(*b*) has been exposed to the infection of any such disease.

(2) This section applies to such diseases of animals as may from time to time be directed by order of the Ministers.

(3) The Minister shall pay for animals slaughtered under this section compensation of such amount as may be determined in accordance with scales prescribed by order of the Minister made with the Treasury's approval.

A statutory instrument containing an order under this sub-section shall be subject to annulment in pursuance of a resolution of either House of Parliament.

(4) This section does not apply to poultry ; and in this section—

(*a*) " animals " includes horses ;

(*b*) " disease " is not restricted by its definition in this Act.

33. The Minister may, for the purposes of his powers under   PART II
this Act relating to the slaughter by him of animals, employ Additional
such additional inspectors, valuers and other persons, and at staff and
such remuneration, and may incur such expenses, as, subject expenses.
to the approval of the Minister for the Civil Service, he thinks
necessary.

34.—(1) The Minister may, notwithstanding anything in this Slaughter and
Act, reserve for observation and treatment an animal liable to compensation
be slaughtered under this Act at his direction but subject to generally.
payment of compensation by him as in case of actual slaughter.

(2) Where an animal has been slaughtered under this Act
at the Minister's direction, the carcase of the animal shall
belong to the Minister and shall be buried, or sold, or otherwise
disposed of by him, or as he directs, as the condition of the
animal or carcase and other circumstances may require or
admit.

(3) If, in any case, the sum received by the Minister on sale
of a carcase under this section exceeds the amount paid for
compensation to the owner of the animal slaughtered, he shall
pay that excess to the owner, after deducting reasonable
expenses.

(4) Where an animal has been slaughtered under this Act
at the Minister's direction, he may use for the burial of the
carcase any ground in the possession or occupation of the owner
of the animal and suitable in that behalf, or any common or
unenclosed land.

(5) If the owner of an animal slaughtered under this Act at
the Minister's direction has an insurance on the animal, the
amount of the compensation awarded to him under this Act
may be deducted by the insurers from the amount of the money
payable under the insurance before they make any payment in
respect of it.

(6) Notwithstanding anything in this Act, the Minister may, if
he thinks fit, withhold, either wholly or partially, compensation
or other payment in respect of an animal slaughtered under this
Act at his discretion, where the animal, being an imported
animal, was in his judgment diseased at the time of its landing
or, before or while being brought from a member State, exposed
to the infection of disease.

(7) The Ministers may make such orders as they think fit for
all or any of the following purposes—

    (*a*) for prescribing the mode of ascertainment of the value
        of an animal slaughtered, or liable to be slaughtered, at
        their direction ;

    (*b*) for regulating applications for, and the mode of payment
        of, compensation ;

A 9

(c) for prescribing and regulating the destruction, burial, disposal or treatment of carcases of animals slaughtered at their direction,

and they may by order provide that subsection (6) above shall cease to have effect.

Carcases etc. liable to spread disease

35.—(1) The Ministers may by order make such provision—

(a) for the seizure of carcases, fodder, litter, eggs, milk, skim milk, whey, buttermilk, cream or fertilisers, and

(b) for the destruction, burial, disposal or treatment of anything seized under the order,

as they may think expedient for preventing the spread of any disease to which this subsection applies.

(2) Subsection (1) above applies to the diseases in the case of which powers of slaughter are exercisable under this Act, that is to say—

(a) to cattle plague, pleuro-pneumonia, foot-and-mouth disease and swine-fever, and any disease within the meaning of section 32 above to which that section for the time being applies; and

(b) to any disease as defined in relation to poultry by or under section 88 below.

(3) The Ministers may make such orders as they think fit—

(a) for prescribing and regulating the destruction, burial, disposal or treatment of carcases of animals dying while diseased or suspected;

(b) for prescribing and regulating the destruction, burial or disposal of anything seized under subsection (1);

(c) for prohibiting or regulating the digging up of carcases which have been buried.

(4) A person is guilty of an offence against this Act who, without lawful authority or excuse, proof of which shall lie on him—

(a) throws or places, or causes or suffers to be thrown or placed, into any river, stream, canal, navigation, or other water, or into the sea within 4.8 kilometres of the shore, the carcase of an animal which has died of disease, or been slaughtered as diseased or suspected; or

(b) digs up, or causes to be dug up, a carcase buried under the direction of the Minister or of a local authority or of a receiver of wreck.

36.—(1) The Minister shall pay compensation—

    (*a*) for anything seized under an order made by virtue of section 35(1) above for the purpose of preventing the spread of foot-and-mouth disease ;

    (*b*) for anything seized under such an order for the purpose of preventing the spread of any other disease to which section 35(1) applies, except the carcase of any animal or bird affected with that disease.

(2) The Ministers may by order provide for the payment by the Minister of compensation for carcases seized as mentioned above of animals or birds affected with any disease to which section 35(1) applies other than foot-and-mouth disease or fowl pest.

(3) The compensation payable under subsection (1) or subsection (2) above for anything seized shall be its value at the time of seizure.

(4) Where anything destroyed, buried or disposed of under an order made under paragraph (*e*) of section 23 above could have been seized under an order made under section 35(1), the Minister shall pay the like compensation (if any) for it as if it had been so seized at the time of the destruction, burial or disposal.

(5) The Ministers may make such orders as they think fit for all or any of the following purposes—

    (*a*) for prescribing how the value of anything seized under section 35(1) is to be ascertained ;

    (*b*) for regulating applications for, and the mode of payment of, any compensation payable by virtue of this section ;

    (*c*) for prescribing and regulating the destruction, burial or disposal of anything seized under section 35(1).

PART III

WELFARE AND EXPORT

Care

37.—(1) The Ministers may make such orders as they think fit for the purpose of protecting animals from unnecessary suffering—

    (*a*) during inland transit, including transit by an aircraft on a flight beginning and ending in Great Britain ; or

    (*b*) while exposed for sale ; or

    (*c*) while awaiting removal after being exposed for sale.

(2) The Ministers may make such orders as they think fit—

 (*a*) for ensuring for animals carried by sea or by air proper ventilation during the passage and on landing; and

 (*b*) for protecting them from unnecessary suffering during the passage and on landing.

Food and water.

38.—(1) The Ministers may make such orders as they think fit for ensuring for animals a proper supply of food and water —

 (*a*) for any period in which the animals are detained ; and

 (*b*) during their passage by sea or by air and on landing.

(2) The following bodies—

1962 c. 46.

 (*a*) The Boards established by the Transport Act 1962,

 (*b*) the London Transport Executive, and

 (*c*) every railway company,

shall to the satisfaction of the appropriate Minister provide food and water, or either of them, at such railway stations as the appropriate Minister by general or specific description directs, for animals carried, or about to be or having been carried, on the railway of any of those bodies, and the additional provisions of Schedule 4 to this Act have effect accordingly.

In this subsection and in Schedule 4—

 (i) references to the bodies mentioned in paragraphs (*a*) and (*b*) include wholly-owned subsidiaries of those bodies ;

 (ii) " railway company " includes a person working a railway under lease or otherwise.

Export

Export of animals generally.

39.—(1) The Ministers may by order provide in the interests of animal welfare for regulating the exportation from Great Britain of animals, and in particular—

 (*a*) for prohibiting exportation without such certificate or licence as may be prescribed by the order ; and

 (*b*) as to the circumstances in which and conditions on which a certificate or licence may be obtained.

(2) Without prejudice to the generality of subsection (1) above, an order under this section may include provision for requiring persons proposing to export animals from Great Britain to furnish information about—

 (*a*) the intended ultimate destination of the animals ;

 (*b*) the arrangements for conveying them to that destination ; and

 (*c*) any other matters which may be specified in the order.

Export of horses other than those defined as ponies

40.—(1) It is an offence against this Act to ship or attempt Restriction on
to ship any horse (which for the purpose of this section does export of
not include a horse defined by this Act to be a pony) in any horses.
vessel or aircraft from any port or aerodrome in Great Britain
to any port or aerodrome outside the British Islands unless the
horse—

   (*a*) immediately before shipment has been examined by a
       veterinary inspector appointed by the Minister for the
       purpose of conducting examinations under this section,
       and

   (*b*) has been certified in writing by the inspector to comply
       with the conditions mentioned in subsection (2) below,

but this subsection shall not apply in such cases as may be
prescribed by order of the Ministers.

A statutory instrument containing an order under this subsection shall be subject to annulment in pursuance of a resolution
of either House of Parliament.

(2) The conditions referred to in subsection (1) above are that
the horse—

   (*a*) is capable of being conveyed to the port or aerodrome
       outside the British Islands and disembarked without
       cruelty ; and

   (*b*) is capable of being worked without suffering.

(3) Where the inspector is satisfied that the horse is of one
of the categories set out in the first column of the following table
the conditions to be complied with shall include the condition
that in the inspector's opinion the horse—

   (*a*) is not more than 8 years of age ; and

   (*b*) is of not less value than the amount specified in respect
       of it in the second column of that table, or such other
       amount as may be prescribed by order of the Ministers.

TABLE

	£
A heavy draft horse	715
A vanner, mule or jennet	495
An ass	220

(4) Subsection (3) above shall not apply in the case of any
horse where the inspector is satisfied—

   (*a*) that it is intended to use the horse as a performing
       animal ; or

   (*b*) that the horse is registered in the stud book of a society
       for the encouragement of horse-breeding recognised by
       the Ministers, and is intended to be used for breeding
       or exhibition ; or

(*c*) that the horse is a foal at foot accompanying such a horse as is referred to in paragraph (*b*) above.

Export of horses defined as ponies

Restriction on export of ponies.

41.—(1) It is an offence against this Act to ship or attempt to ship any pony in any vessel or aircraft from any port or aerodrome in Great Britain to any port or aerodrome outside the British Islands unless—

(*a*) the appropriate Minister is satisfied that the pony is intended for breeding, riding or exhibition and—

(i) it is not of less value than £300, or

(ii) in the case of a pony not exceeding 122 centimetres in height other than a pony of the Shetland breed not exceeding 107 centimetres in height, it is not of less value than £220, or

(iii) in the case of such a pony of the Shetland breed, it is not of less value than £145, or

(iv) such other value in any of those cases as may be prescribed by order of the Ministers; and

(*b*) immediately before shipment the pony has been individually inspected by a veterinary inspector and has been certified in writing by the inspector to be capable of being conveyed to the port or aerodrome to which it is to be shipped, and disembarked, without unnecessary suffering.

(2) Without prejudice to paragraph (*b*) of subsection (1) above, a veterinary inspector shall not certify a pony to be capable of being conveyed and disembarked as described in that subsection if—

(*a*) being a mare, it is in his opinion heavy in foal, showing fullness of udder or too old to travel; or

(*b*) being a foal, it is in his opinion too young to travel.

Restriction on export of registered ponies.

42. It is an offence against this Act to ship or attempt to ship a registered pony in any vessel or aircraft from any port or aerodrome in Great Britain to any port or aerodrome outside the British Islands unless there has first been obtained from the secretary of a society in whose stud book the pony is registered a certificate (" the export certificate ") that the pony is registered with that society.

For the purposes of this section the expression " registered pony " means a pony registered in—

(*a*) the Arab Horse Society Stud Book,

(*b*) the National Pony Society Stud Book,

(*c*) the British Palomino Society Stud Book, or

(d) the British Spotted Horse and Pony Society Stud Book, PART III
or in the stud book of any of the following native breed societies, namely, English Connemara, Dales, Dartmoor, Exmoor, Fell, Highland, New Forest, Shetland and Welsh.

43. The Ministers shall by order make such provision as they Regulation of think necessary or expedient for the following purposes— export of
ponies.

    (a) for prohibiting the export of ponies by sea or air from any place in Great Britain to any place outside the British Islands unless such ponies are rested immediately before being loaded in the vessel or aircraft in which they are to be carried ;

    (b) for regulating and prescribing the premises at which and the periods during which ponies are to be so rested ;

    (c) for prescribing and regulating the cleansing and supervision of such premises and the provision at them of clean and sufficient bedding and adequate supplies of fodder and water.

Other provisions as to export of horses

44. If any horse examined under section 40(1) above or Slaughter on inspected under section 41(1) above is found by the veterinary examination of inspector— inspection.

    (a) to be in such a physical condition that it is cruel to keep it alive, or

    (b) to be permanently incapable of being worked without suffering,

the inspector shall forthwith slaughter it (or cause it to be slaughtered) with a mechanically operated instrument suitable and sufficient for the purpose, and no compensation shall be made to the owner of that animal.

45.—(1) A veterinary inspector may, for the purposes of Marking of identification, mark a horse certified by him under section 40(1) horses above or section 41(1) above in such manner as the Ministers certified for
export. may by order prescribe.

(2) A person who, with a view to evading the provisions of section 40 above or section 41 above, marks a horse—

    (a) with the prescribed mark, or

    (b) with any mark so nearly resembling it as to be calculated to deceive,

is guilty of an offence against this Act.

46.—(1) If any horse shipped from any port in Great Britain Slaughter of to any port outside the British Islands has a limb broken or is injured horses.

PART III   otherwise seriously injured while on board so as to be incapable of being disembarked without cruelty—

> (*a*) the master of the vessel shall forthwith cause the animal to be slaughtered ; and
>
> (*b*) every vessel on which a horse is so shipped shall carry a proper killing instrument, to be approved by the Ministers for that purpose.

(2) It is the duty of the owner and master of every such vessel to see that the vessel is provided with such an instrument, and the master, if so required by an inspector, shall produce the instrument for his inspection.

Exemption of thoroughbreds in transit.   **47.** Sections 40 and 41 and 46 above shall not apply in the case of shipment of any thoroughbred horse certified in writing by a steward or the secretary of the Jockey Club—

> (*a*) to have arrived in Great Britain not more than one month before the date of shipment for the purpose of being run in a race ; or
>
> (*b*) to be shipped for the purpose of being run in a race ; or
>
> (*c*) to be shipped in order to be used for breeding purposes.

Certificates.   **48.** Where—

> (*a*) a certificate is given under section 40(1), section 41(1) or section 47 above, or
>
> (*b*) an export certificate is given under section 42 above,

that certificate shall be delivered at the time of shipment to the master of the vessel or the pilot of the aircraft on which the animal is shipped, who shall—

> (i) on demand produce the certificate to any constable or any inspector or other officer of the appropriate Minister or the local authority ; and
>
> (ii) allow such constable, inspector or other officer to take a copy of or extract from the certificate.

Enforcement and interpretation.   **49.**—(1) An inspector may enter any vessel or aircraft for the purpose of ascertaining whether the provisions—

> (*a*) of sections 40 to 42 and 44 to 48 above (in this section described as " the relevant sections "), or
>
> (*b*) of any order under this Act relating to the exportation or shipment of horses,

are being complied with.

(2) Every local authority shall, if and so far as the Ministers by order so direct, execute and enforce the relevant sections.

(3) If—

    (*a*) a person does anything or omits to do anything in contravention of the provisions of the relevant sections, or

    (*b*) the master of a vessel or the pilot of an aircraft permits a horse to be shipped in a vessel or aircraft in contravention of those provisions,

he shall be guilty of an offence against this Act, and the provisions of this Act relating to offences and legal proceedings shall apply accordingly as if the expression " animal " in those provisions included horses.

(4) In this section and the relevant sections—

    (*a*) " master ", " owner ", " port ", and " vessel " have the same meanings as in the Merchant Shipping Act 1894 ; 1894 c. 60. and

    (*b*) " pilot of an aircraft " includes any other person having the command or charge of the aircraft.

PART IV

LOCAL AUTHORITIES

50.—(1) In this Act " local authority " has the meaning given by subsections (2) and (3) below, but subject to subsection (4) below.

Local authorities for purposes of this Act.

(2) In the application of this Act to England and Wales " local authority " means—

    (*a*) as respects a London borough, the borough council,

    (*b*) as respects each county, the county council,

and the Common Council of the City of London shall be the local authority—

        (i) for the City of London, and

        (ii) in and for the whole of Greater London for the purpose of the provisions of this Act relating to imported animals.

(3) In the application of this Act to Scotland " local authority " means a regional or islands council.

(4) Where the district or part of a district of a local authority is or comprises, or is comprised in—

    (*a*) a port or part of a port, or

    (*b*) an aerodrome or part of an aerodrome,

the appropriate Minister may, if he thinks fit, in relation to either paragraph (*a*) or paragraph (*b*) above by order make any body, other than the local authority under subsection (2) or subsection (3) above, the local authority for the purposes of the provisions of this Act relating to imported animals.

(5) A local authority shall execute and enforce this Act and every order of the Minister so far as they are to be executed and enforced by local authorities.

Local authorities and their districts.

51.—(1) The provisions of this Act conferring powers on, or otherwise relating to, a local authority, or their inspectors or officers shall, unless otherwise expressed, be read as having reference to the district of the local authority.

(2) The powers so conferred shall, unless it is otherwise expressed, be exercisable and shall operate within and in relation to that district only.

Inspectors and other officers.

52.—(1) Every local authority shall appoint as many inspectors and other officers as the local authority think necessary for the execution and enforcement of this Act.

(2) Every local authority shall assign to those inspectors and officers such duties, and salaries or allowances, and may delegate to any of them such authorities and discretion, as to the local authority seem fit, and may at any time revoke any appointment so made.

Borrowing powers.

53.—(1) A local authority may borrow for the purposes of this Act.

(2) In Scotland the power conferred by this section shall only be exercisable where the expenditure of the local authority under this Act requiring to be met out of rates in any financial year exceeds or would exceed the produce of a rate of 2½p. in the pound on the rateable valuation of the authority's area.

Provision of wharves etc.

54.—(1) A local authority may provide, erect and fit up wharves, stations, lairs, sheds and other places for the landing, reception, keeping, sale, slaughter or disposal of imported or other animals, carcases, fodder, litter, dung and other things.

1847 c. 14.

(2) There shall be incorporated with this Act the Markets and Fairs Clauses Act 1847, except sections 6 to 9, and 52 to 59.

(3) A wharf or other place provided by a local authority under this section shall be a market within that Act, and this Act shall be the special Act; and

    (*a*) the prescribed limits shall be the limits of lands acquired or appropriated for the purposes of this section;

    (*b*) byelaws shall be approved by the appropriate Minister, which approval shall be sufficient without any other approval or allowance where—

        (i) notice of application for approval has been given, and

        (ii) the proposed byelaws have been published before application,

    as required by that Act of 1847.

(4) A local authority may charge for the use of a wharf or other place provided by them under this section such sums as may be imposed by byelaws, and those sums shall be deemed tolls authorised by the special Act.

(5) All sums so received by a local authority in England or Wales—

(a) shall be carried to a separate account ; and

(b) shall be applied in payment of interest and repayment of principal in respect of money borrowed by them under this Act ; and

(c) subject to paragraph (b), shall be applied towards the discharge of their expenses under this Act.

(6) The local authority shall make such periodical returns to the appropriate Minister as he may require of their expenditure and receipts in respect of the wharf or other place.

55.—(1) A local authority may— Power to acquire land.

(a) purchase land by agreement, or

(b) if so authorised by the Minister or the appropriate Minister, purchase land compulsorily, or

(c) by agreement take land on lease or at a rent,

for the following purposes—

(i) for wharves or other places ; or

(ii) for use for burial of carcases, in cases where there is not any ground suitable in that behalf in the possession or occupation of the owner of the animal, or any common or unenclosed land suitable and approved by the Minister or the appropriate Minister in that behalf ; or

(iii) for any other purpose of this Act.

(2) The powers conferred by this section may be exercised by a local authority in England or Wales with respect to land within or without their district.

(3) References in the Acquisition of Land (Authorisation Procedure) Act 1946 and the Acquisition of Land (Authorisation Procedure) (Scotland) Act 1947 to enactments in force immediately before the respective commencements of those Acts shall include references to this section. 1946 c. 49.
1947 c. 42.

This subsection is without prejudice to paragraph (a) of section 17(2) of the Interpretation Act 1978 as regards references in an Act to an enactment repealed and re-enacted. 1978 c. 30.

56.—(1) A local authority may provide, fit up and maintain portable dipping tanks or dipping places, and afford their use, Public facilities for sheep dipping.

PART IV   and the use of all necessary connected appliances and materials, to the public upon such terms and conditions as the local authority may think fit.

(2) Any sums received by a local authority in England or Wales for such use shall be applied by them towards the discharge of their expenses under this Act.

(3) No dipping place shall be used for the purposes of this section if such use would injuriously affect the water in any stream, reservoir, aqueduct, well, pond or place constructed or used for the supply of water for drinking or other domestic purposes.

Burial of carcases washed ashore.   **57.**—(1) Where a carcase washed ashore is buried or destroyed under the direction of a receiver of wreck with authority from the Secretary of State the expenses of such burial or destruction shall be expenses of the local authority.

(2) Those expenses shall be paid by the local authority to the receiver on demand, and in default of payment shall be recoverable with costs by the receiver from the local authority.

(3) Where a local authority has incurred any expenses under this section on account of the burial or destruction of the carcase of any animal which, or the carcase of which, was thrown or washed from any vessel, the owner of the vessel shall be liable to repay such expenses to the local authority.

Regulations.   **58.**—(1) A regulation of a local authority may be proved—

    (*a*) by the production of a newspaper purporting to contain the regulation as an advertisement ; or

    (*b*) by the production of a copy of the regulation purporting to be certified by the clerk of the local authority as a true copy.

(2) A regulation so proved shall be taken to have been duly made, unless and until the contrary is proved.

(3) A regulation of a local authority authorised by this Act or by an order of the Minister shall alone be deemed for the purposes of this Act a regulation of a local authority.

Default.   **59.**—(1) Where a local authority fail to execute or enforce any of the provisions of this Act, or of an order of the Minister, the appropriate Minister may by order empower a person named in that order—

    (*a*) to execute and enforce those provisions ; or

    (*b*) to procure their execution and enforcement.

(2) The expenses incurred under any such order or in respect of any such default by or on behalf of the appropriate Minister shall be expenses of the local authority, and

(*a*) the treasurer or other proper officer of the local authority shall pay the amount of such expenses to the appropriate Minister on demand ; and

(*b*) in default of payment a person appointed by the appropriate Minister to sue in that behalf may recover the amount of such expenses from the local authority.

(3) For the purposes of this section an order of the Minister shall be conclusive in respect of any default, amount of expenses, or other matter stated or appearing in it.

(4) The provisions of this section are without prejudice to the right or power of the appropriate Minister, or any other authority or any person, to take any other proceedings for requiring a local authority to execute or enforce any of the provisions of this Act or of an order of the Minister.

PART V

ENFORCEMENT, OFFENCES AND PROCEEDINGS

Enforcement

60.—(1) The police force of each police area shall execute and enforce this Act and every order of the Minister.

Duties and authorities of constables.

(2) Where a person is seen or found committing, or is reasonably suspected of being engaged in committing, an offence against this Act, a constable may, without warrant, stop and detain him.

(3) If that person's name and address are not known to the constable, and he fails to give them to the constable's satisfaction, the constable may, without warrant, apprehend him.

(4) The constable may, whether so stopping or detaining or apprehending the person or not—

(*a*) stop, detain and examine any animal, vehicle, boat or thing to which the offence or suspected offence relates ; and

(*b*) require it to be forthwith taken back to or into any place or district from which or out of which it was unlawfully removed and execute and enforce that requisition.

(5) If a person obstructs or impedes or assists in obstructing or impeding a constable or other officer in the execution—

(*a*) of this Act, or

(*b*) of an order of the Minister, or

(*c*) of a regulation of a local authority,

the constable or officer may without warrant apprehend the offender.

(6) A person apprehended under this section—

> (*a*) shall be taken with all practicable speed before a justice, or, in Scotland, a sheriff or district court; and

> (*b*) shall not be detained without a warrant longer than is necessary for that purpose.

(7) All enactments relating to the release of persons on bail by an officer of police or a constable shall apply in the case of a person apprehended under this section.

(8) The foregoing provisions of this section respecting a constable extend and apply to any person called by a constable to his assistance.

(9) A constable shall forthwith make a report in writing to his superior officer of every case in which he stops any person, animal, vehicle, boat, or thing under this section, and of his proceedings in consequence.

(10) Nothing in this section shall take away or abridge any power or authority that a constable would have had if this section had not been enacted.

Powers of
arrest as to
rabies.

61.—(1) Without prejudice to the powers of arrest conferred by section 60 above or otherwise, a constable may arrest without warrant any person whom he, with reasonable cause, suspects to be in the act of committing or to have committed an offence to which this section applies.

(2) The offences to which this section applies are offences against this Act consisting of—

> (*a*) the landing or attempted landing of any animal in contravention of an order made under this Act and expressed to be made for the purpose of preventing the introduction of rabies into Great Britain; or

> (*b*) the failure by the person having the charge or control of any vessel or boat to discharge any obligation imposed on him in that capacity by such an order; or

> (*c*) the movement, in contravention of an order under section 17 or section 23 above, of any animal into, within or out of a place or area declared to be infected with rabies.

Entry and
search under
s. 61.

62.—(1) For the purpose of arresting a person under the power conferred by section 61 above a constable may enter (if need be, by force) and search any vessel, boat, aircraft or vehicle of any other description in which that person is or in which the constable, with reasonable cause, suspects him to be.

(2) For the purpose of exercising any power to seize an animal or cause an animal to be seized, and—

    (*a*) where that power is conferred on constables by an order made under this Act, and

    (*b*) where that power is expressed to be made for the purpose of preventing the introduction of rabies into Great Britain.

a constable may enter (if need be, by force) and search any vessel, boat, aircraft or vehicle of any other description in which there is, or in which he, with reasonable cause, suspects that there is, an animal to which that power applies.

63.—(1) An inspector has— General powers of inspectors.

    (*a*) for the purposes of this Act, but

    (*b*) with the exception of the powers conferred by sections 61 and 62 above,

all the powers which a constable has, under this Act or otherwise, in the place where the inspector is acting.

(2) An inspector may at any time enter any land or shed to which this Act applies, or other building or place where he has reasonable grounds for supposing—

    (*a*) that disease exists or has within 56 days existed ; or

    (*b*) that the carcase of a diseased or suspected animal is or has been kept, or has been buried, destroyed, or otherwise disposed of ; or

    (*c*) that there is to be found any pen, place, vehicle, or thing in respect of which any person has on any occasion failed to comply with the provisions of this Act, or of an order of the Minister, or of a regulation of a local authority ; or

    (*d*) that this Act or an order of the Minister or a regulation of a local authority has not been or is not being complied with.

(3) An inspector may at any time enter any pen, vehicle, vessel, boat or aircraft in which or where he has reasonable grounds for supposing that this Act or an order of the Minister or a regulation of a local authority has not been or is not being complied with.

(4) An inspector entering as authorised by the foregoing provisions of this section shall, if required by the owner, or occupier, or person in charge of the land, building, place, pen, vehicle, vessel, boat or aircraft state in writing his reasons for entering.

(5) For the purpose of ascertaining whether the provisions of any order under section 10 above or the conditions of any licence

issued in accordance with any such order are being complied with, an inspector may at any time enter—

    (*a*) any vessel, boat, aircraft or vehicle of any other description which is for the time being within the limits of a port, within the meaning of the Customs and Excise Management Act 1979, or at a customs and excise airport, within the meaning of that Act ; or

    (*b*) any vessel, boat or aircraft which does not fall within paragraph (*a*) above but which he has reasonable grounds for supposing has recently been brought into Great Britain.

(6) Without prejudice to subsection (5) above, an inspector may at any time enter—

    (*a*) any land, building or other place, or

    (*b*) any vessel, boat, aircraft or vehicle of any other description,

on or in which he has reasonable grounds for supposing that there is being or has been kept any animal or other thing which has been imported and the importation of which is for the time being prohibited or regulated by an order under section 10 ; and in this subsection " animals " and " imported " have the same meaning as in that section.

(7) A certificate of a veterinary inspector to the effect that an animal is or was affected with a disease specified in the certificate shall, for the purposes of this Act, be conclusive evidence in all courts of justice of the matter certified.

(8) An inspector of the Minister has all the powers of an inspector throughout Great Britain or that part for which he is appointed.

(9) In addition to the powers conferred by this section upon inspectors, an inspector of the Minister may at any time, for the purpose of ascertaining whether pleuro-pneumonia, foot-and-mouth disease or swine-fever exists, or has within 56 days existed, in any shed, land or other place, enter such shed, land or place.

Powers of
inspectors as
to poultry.

64.—(1) An inspector of the Ministry and, if so authorised by an order of the Minister, an inspector of a local authority, may at any time enter any pen, shed, land or other place in which he has reasonable grounds for supposing that poultry are or have been kept, for the purpose of ascertaining whether disease exists or has existed in or on them.

(2) For the purpose of enforcing any order for protecting poultry from unnecessary suffering, an inspector may examine—

    (*a*) poultry in any circumstances to which the order relates, and (*b*) any receptacle or vehicle used for their conveyance or exposure for sale,

and he may enter any premises, vessel or aircraft in which he has reasonable ground for supposing that there are poultry—

      (i) exposed for sale ; or

      (ii) in course of conveyance ; or

      (iii) packed for conveyance or exposure for sale.

65.—(1) Where an inspector of the Minister is satisfied that this Act or an order of the Minister or a regulation of a local authority has not been or is not being complied with on board a vessel in port, then, on the inspector's representation in writing to that effect, stating particulars of non-compliance, the vessel may be detained until the appropriate Minister otherwise directs.

  Power to detain vessels and aircraft.

(2) The officer detaining the vessel shall forthwith deliver to the master or person in charge of the vessel a copy of the representation.

(3) Section 692 of the Merchant Shipping Act 1894 shall apply in the case of such detention as if it were authorised or ordered under that Act.

  1894 c. 60.

(4) In relation to aircraft the Ministers may—

  (*a*) by an order under this Act adapt that section of the 1894 Act as applied in the case of the detention of a vessel under this section ; or

  (*b*) make such other provision instead of it as they think expedient.

66. A person is guilty of an offence against this Act who, without lawful authority or excuse, proof of which shall lie on him—

  Refusal and obstruction.

  (*a*) refuses to an inspector or other officer, acting in execution of this Act, or of an order of the Minister, or of a regulation of a local authority, admission to any land, building, place, pen, vessel, boat, aircraft or vehicle of any other description which the inspector or officer is entitled to enter or examine ; or

  (*b*) obstructs or impedes him in so entering or examining ; or (*c*) otherwise in any respect obstructs or impedes an inspector or constable or other officer in the execution of his duty, or assists in any such obstructing or impeding.

Offences as to licences, declarations, certificates and instruments

Issue of false licences etc.

67. A person is guilty of an offence against this Act—

(*a*) who grants or issues a licence, certificate or instrument made or issued, or purporting to be made or issued under or for any purpose of this Act, or of an order of the Minister, or of a regulation of a local authority, which is false in any date or other material particular, unless he shows to the court's satisfaction that he did not know of that falsity, and that he could not with reasonable diligence have obtained knowledge of it ; or

(*b*) who grants or issues such a licence, certificate or instrument not having, and knowing that he has not, lawful authority to grant or issue it.

Issue of licences etc. in blank.

68. A person is guilty of an offence against this Act—

(*a*) who, with intent unlawfully to evade or defeat this Act, or an order of the Minister, or a regulation of a local authority, grants or issues an instrument being in form a licence, certificate or instrument made or issued under this Act, or such an order or regulation, for permitting or regulating the movement of a particular animal, or the doing of any other particular thing, but being issued in blank, that is to say, not being before its issue so filled up as to specify any particular animal or thing ;

(*b*) who uses or offers or attempts to use for any purpose of this Act, or such an order or regulation, an instrument so issued in blank, unless he shows to the court's satisfaction that he did not know of it having been so issued in blank, and that he could not with reasonable diligence have obtained knowledge of it.

Falsely obtaining licences etc.

69. A person is guilty of an offence against this Act—

(*a*) who for the purpose of obtaining a licence, certificate or instrument makes a declaration or statement false in any material particular, or

(*b*) who obtains or endeavours to obtain a licence, certificate or instrument by means of a false pretence,

unless he shows to the court's satisfaction that he did not know of that falsity, and that he could not with reasonable diligence have obtained knowledge of it.

70. A person is guilty of an offence against this Act, who, with intent unlawfully to evade this Act, or an order of the Minister, or a regulation of a local authority—

    (*a*) alters, or falsely makes, or ante-dates, or counterfeits a licence, declaration, certificate or instrument made or issued, or purporting to be made or issued, under or for any purpose of this Act or such an order or regulation ; or

    (*b*) offers or utters such a licence, declaration, certificate or instrument knowing it to be altered, or falsely made, or ante-dated or counterfeited.

71. A person is guilty of an offence against this Act—

    (*a*) who, with intent unlawfully to evade this Act, or an order of the Minister, or a regulation of a local authority, does anything for which a licence is requisite under this Act, or such an order or regulation, without having obtained a licence ; or

    (*b*) who, where a licence is so requisite, having obtained a licence, with the like intent does the thing licensed after the licence has expired ; or

    (*c*) who uses or offers or attempts to use as such a licence—

        (i) an instrument not being a complete licence, or

        (ii) an instrument untruly purporting or appearing to be a licence,

unless he shows to the court's satisfaction that he did not know of that incompleteness or untruth, and that he could not with reasonable diligence have obtained knowledge of it.

Offences generally

72. A person is guilty of an offence against this Act who, without lawful authority or excuse, proof of which shall lie on him—

    (*a*) does or omits anything the doing or omission of which is declared by this Act or by an order of the Minister to be an offence by that person against this Act ; or

    (*b*) does anything which by this Act or such an order is made or declared to be not lawful.

73. A person is guilty of an offence against this Act who, without lawful authority or excuse, proof of which shall lie on him—

    (*a*) does anything in contravention of this Act, or of an order of the Minister, or of a regulation of a local authority ; or (*b*) fails to give, produce, observe or do any notice, licence, rule or thing which by this Act or such an order or regulation he is required to give, produce, observe or do.

Further provisions as to punishment of offences

Liability
under the
customs and
excise Acts.

74. A person who—

(*a*) lands or ships or attempts to land or ship an animal or thing, and

(*b*) by so doing is in contravention of this Act or of an order of the Minister,

is liable under and according to the customs and excise Acts to the penalties imposed on persons importing or exporting or attempting to import or export goods the importation or exportation of which is prohibited.

This section is without prejudice to any proceeding under this Act against such a person for an offence against this Act.

Punishment
of summary
offences not
otherwise
provided for.

75.—(1) A person guilty of an offence against this Act for which a penalty is not provided by any other provision of this Act shall be liable on summary conviction—

(*a*) to a fine not exceeding £400 ; or

(*b*) if the offence is committed with respect to more than 10 animals, to a fine not exceeding £50 for each animal ; or

(*c*) where the offence is committed in relation to carcases, fodder, litter, dung or other thing (exclusive of animals), to a fine not exceeding £50 in respect of every 508 kilogrammes in weight thereof after the first 508 kilogrammes in addition to the first fine not exceeding £400.

(2) An order—

(*a*) made under this Act, and

(*b*) expressed to be made for the purpose of preventing the introduction or spreading of rabies into or within Great Britain,

may direct that paragraph (*a*) of subsection (1) above shall have effect in relation to any summary offence against this Act the existence of which is attributable to the provisions of that order as if for " £400 " there were substituted " £1,000 ".

(3) That paragraph (*a*) of subsection (1) shall have effect as provided by subsection (2) above in relation to any summary

offence the existence of which is attributable to the provisions of
either of the following orders—

    (*a*) Rabies (Importation of Dogs, Cats and Other Mammals) S.I. 1974/2211.
        Order 1974 ; and

    (*b*) Rabies (Control) Order 1974.   S.I. 1974/2212.

    (4) A person convicted of an offence under any of the following provisions of this Act—

    section 15(7),

    paragraph (*a*) of section 35(4),

    section 66,

    section 72, and

    section 73,

is liable in the court's discretion on a further conviction for a second or subsequent offence against the same provision to imprisonment for any term not exceeding one month in lieu of the fine to which he is liable under subsection (1) above.

    (5) A person convicted of an offence under any of the following provisions of this Act—

    section 8(2),

    paragraph (*b*) of section 35(4),

    section 67,

    section 68,

    section 69,

    section 70, and

    section 71,

is liable in the court's discretion to imprisonment for any term not exceeding 2 months in lieu of the fine to which he is liable under subsection (1) above.

    (6) Nothing in this section applies in relation to an offence punishable under section 4 above.

    76.—(1) Where—

    (*a*) an offence against this Act which is declared to be such   Certain
        by an order under section 10 above, and   importation
            offences
    (*b*) that order is expressed to be made for the purpose of   triable either
        preventing the introduction of rabies into Great Britain,   summarily or
that offence may be tried either summarily or on indictment.   on indictment.

    (2) For an offence triable under subsection (1) above a person shall be liable—

    (*a*) on summary conviction to a fine not exceeding the statutory maximum ;

   (*b*) on conviction on indictment to a fine or to imprisonment for a term not exceeding 12 months or to both.

(3) Where an order under section 10 declares that this sub-section applies to an offence which consists of—

   (*a*) a contravention of, or failure to comply with, any provision of that order, or

   (*b*) a failure to observe any conditions to which a licence issued in accordance with that order is subject,

that offence may be tried either summarily or on indictment, and a person convicted of such an offence shall be liable as provided in paragraphs (*a*) and (*b*) of subsection (2) above.

(4) In this section " the statutory maximum ", in relation to a fine on summary conviction, means—

1980 c. 43.   (*a*) in England and Wales, the prescribed sum within the meaning of section 32 of the Magistrates' Courts Act 1980 (at the passing of this Act £1000) ;

1975 c. 21.   (*b*) in Scotland, the prescribed sum within the meaning of section 289B of the Criminal Procedure (Scotland) Act 1975 (at the passing of this Act £1000).

Until the coming into force of the Magistrates' Courts Act 1980 any reference in this subsection to any provision of that Act shall have effect as if it were a reference to the corresponding
1977 c. 45.   provision of the Criminal Law Act 1977.

Proceedings

Money recoverable summarily.   **77.** Any money by this Act or an order of the Minister made recoverable summarily may be so recovered as a civil debt, and in England and Wales this shall be in accordance with the Magistrates' Courts Act 1980.

Until the coming into force of the Magistrates' Courts Act 1980 the reference in this section to that Act shall have effect
1952 c. 55.   as if it were a reference to the Magistrates' Courts Act 1952.

Appeal.   **78.** If any person thinks himself aggrieved—

   (*a*) by the dismissal of a complaint by, or

   (*b*) by any determination or adjudication of,

a magistrates' court in England or Wales under this Act, he may appeal to the Crown Court.

Nothing in this section applies in relation to an offence punishable under section 4 above.

Evidence and procedure.   **79.**—(1) In any proceeding under this Act no proof shall be required of the appointment or handwriting of an inspector or other officer of the Minister or of the clerk or an inspector or other officer of a local authority.

(2) Where the owner or person in charge of an animal is charged with an offence against this Act relative to disease or to any illness of the animal, he shall be presumed to have known of the existence of the disease or illness unless and until he shows to the court's satisfaction that—

(a) he had not knowledge of the existence of that disease or illness, and

(b) he could not with reasonable diligence have obtained that knowledge.

(3) Where a person—

(a) is charged with an offence against this Act in not having duly cleansed or disinfected any place, vessel, aircraft, vehicle or thing belonging to him or under his charge, and

(b) a presumption against him on the part of the prosecution is raised,

it shall lie on him to prove the due cleansing and disinfection mentioned in paragraph (a).

(4) Every offence against this Act shall be deemed to have been committed, and every cause of complaint or matter for summary proceeding under this Act or an order of the Minister or regulation of a local authority shall be deemed to have arisen, either in any place—

(a) where it actually was committed or arose ; or

(b) where the person charged or complained of or proceeded against happens to be at the time of the institution or commencement of the charge, complaint or proceeding.

(5) Nothing in subsections (2) to (4) above applies in relation to an offence under section 4 above.

PART VI

SUPPLEMENTAL

Reports and information

80.—(1) The Ministers shall make and lay before both Houses of Parliament not later than 31st March a yearly return stating the proceedings and expenditure under this Act of the Ministers, and, as far as reasonably may be, of all local authorities, in the year ending the previous 31st December. Yearly return to Parliament.

(2) The return shall also—

(a) show the number of imported animals landed and found diseased in that year, specifying separately the different kinds of disease, and the ports and aerodromes of exportation and landing, and the mode of disposal of the animals ; and

(b) contain such other information respecting the operation of this Act as the Ministers think fit.

Reports to Minister.

81. Every local authority and their inspectors and officers shall give to the appropriate Minister such notices, reports, returns and information as he requires.

Information from Agricultural Marketing Boards.
1958 c. 47.

82. Every board administering a scheme under the Agricultural Marketing Act 1958 shall give to the appropriate Minister such information as he may reasonably require for the purposes of his functions under this Act.

Notices, fees, and exemption from stamp duty

Form and service of instruments.

83.—(1) Every notice under this Act or under any order or regulation made under this Act must be in writing.

(2) The Ministers may make such orders as they think fit for prescribing and regulating the form and mode of service or delivery of notices and other instruments.

(3) Any notice or other instrument under this Act or under an order of the Minister or a regulation of a local authority may be served on the person to be affected by it, either—

(a) by its delivery to him personally ; or

(b) by the leaving of it for him at his last known place of abode or business ; or

(c) by the sending of it through the post in a letter addressed to him at his last known place of abode or business.

(4) A notice or other instrument—

(a) to be served on the occupier of any building, land or place, may, except when sent by post, be addressed to him by the designation of the occupier of that building, land or place, without naming or further describing him ; and

(b) where it is to be served on the several occupiers of several buildings, lands or places, may, except when sent by post, be addressed to them collectively by the designation of the occupiers of those several buildings, lands or places, without further naming or describing them, but separate copies of it being served on them severally.

Fees.

84.—(1) The Ministers may by order made with the Treasury's approval prescribe fees to be paid with respect to such business transacted or to be transacted under this Act as may be specified in the Order.

A Statutory instrument containing an order under this subsection shall be subject to annulment in pursuance of a resolution of the Commons House of Parliament.

(2) Where—

    (a) an order under subsection (1) above provides for the
payment of a fee before the transaction of the business
with respect to which it is payable, and

    (b) the business is not transacted or not wholly transacted,

the Minister to whom the fee was paid may, if he thinks fit,
repay the whole or part of the fee.

(3) Where—

    (a) an order under subsection (1) provides for any fee to be
paid on the making of an application in a case where
previously a fee was payable only if the application
was granted, then,

    (b) as respects anything done in pursuance of an applica-
tion made before the coming into operation of the
order, the same fee shall be payable as before the
coming into operation of the order and shall be so
payable at the time at which it would then have been
payable.

85. No stamp duty shall be payable on any appointment, Exemption
certificate, declaration, licence or thing under this Act, or an from stamp
order of the Minister, or a regulation of a local authority.   duty.

Interpretation, functions, and orders etc.

86.—(1) In this Act—   Ministers and
                                                              their functions.
    (a) " the Minister " means, in relation to the whole of
Great Britain, the Minister of Agriculture, Fisheries
and Food, and " Ministry " shall be construed accordingly,

    (b) " the appropriate Minister " means, in relation to Eng-
land, the Minister of Agriculture, Fisheries and Food,
and in relation to Scotland or to Wales, the Secretary
of State,

    (c) " the Ministers " means, in relation to the whole of
Great Britain, the Minister of Agriculture, Fisheries
and Food, the Secretary of State for Scotland and the
Secretary of State for Wales, acting jointly,

but in the case of any function under the following provisions
of this Act—

        (i) section 21, so far as it is applicable in relation
to brucellosis, tuberculosis, dourine or infestation
with maggot of the warble fly,

(ii) any other provision so far as it is applicable in relation to brucellosis, brucellosis melitensis, tuberculosis or infestation of cattle with the maggot of the warble fly,

that function, notwithstanding that it is expressed to be exercisable by the Minister or the Ministers, shall be exercisable only by the appropriate Minister.

(2) The powers and duties conferred and imposed by this Act on the Minister shall be executed and discharged by the Minister in manner provided by the Ministry of Agriculture and Fisheries Acts 1889 to 1919, and this Act.

Meaning of "animals" and "poultry".

87.—(1) In this Act, unless the context otherwise requires, " animals " means—

(*a*) cattle, sheep and goats, and

(*b*) all other ruminating animals and swine,

subject to subsections (2) and (3) below.

(2) The Ministers may by order for all or any of the purposes of this Act extend the definition of " animals " in subsection (1) above so that it shall for those or any of those purposes comprise—

(*a*) any kind of mammal except man ; and

(*b*) any kind of four-footed beast which is not a mammal.

(3) The Ministers may by order for all or any of the purposes of this Act (except so far as it relates to disease) extend the definition of " animals " in subsection (1) so that it shall for those or any of those purposes comprise—

(*a*) fish, reptiles, crustaceans, or

(*b*) other cold-blooded creatures of any species,

not being creatures in respect of which an order can be made under subsection (2) above.

(4) In this Act, subject to subsection (5) below and unless the context otherwise requires, " poultry " means birds of the following species—

(*a*) domestic fowls, turkeys, geese, ducks, guinea-fowls and pigeons, and

(*b*) pheasants and partridges,

and subject to the provisions mentioned below, this Act has effect in relation to poultry as it has effect in relation to animals.

The provisions of this Act referred to above are sections 7(2), 15(5), 31 and paragraph 5 of Schedule 3, and sections 32(4) and 64.

(5) The Ministers may by order for all or any of the purposes of this Act, in so far as it applies to poultry—

    (a) extend the definition of "poultry" in subsection (4) above so that it shall for those or any of those purposes comprise any other species of bird ; or

    (b) restrict that definition so that it shall for those or any of those purposes exclude any of the species of bird mentioned in paragraph (b) of subsection (4).

88.—(1) In this Act, unless the context otherwise requires, "disease" means cattle plague, pleuro-pneumonia, foot-and-mouth disease, sheep-pox, sheep scab, or swine fever, subject to subsection (2) below.

(2) The Ministers may by order for all or any of the purposes of this Act extend the definition of "disease" in subsection (1) above so that it shall for those or any of those purposes comprise any other disease of animals.

(3) In this Act, in so far as it applies to poultry, and unless the context otherwise requires, "disease" means—

    (a) fowl pest in any of its forms, including Newcastle disease and fowl plague ; and

    (b) fowl cholera, infectious bronchitis, infectious laryngotracheitis, pullorum disease, fowl typhoid, fowl pox and fowl paralysis,

subject to subsection (4) below.

(4) The Ministers may by order for all or any of the purposes of this Act—

    (a) extend the definition of "disease" in subsection (3) above so that it shall for those or any of those purposes comprise any other disease of birds ; or

    (b) restrict that definition so that it shall for those or any of those purposes exclude any of the diseases mentioned in paragraph (b) of subsection (3).

89.—(1) In this Act, unless the context otherwise requires—

    "aerodrome" means any area of land or water designed, equipped, set apart or commonly used for affording facilities for the landing and departure of aircraft ;

    "carcase" means the carcase of an animal and includes part of a carcase, and the meat, bones, hide, skin, hooves, offal or other part of an animal, separately or otherwise, or any portion thereof ;

    "cattle" means bulls, cows, steers, heifers, and calves ;

    "cattle plague" means rinderpest or the disease commonly called cattle plague ;

" the customs and excise Acts " has the meaning given by the Customs and Excise Management Act 1979 ;

" diseased " means affected with disease ;

" district ", when used with reference to a local authority, means the area for which the local authority exercises powers under this Act ;

" export quarantine station " has the meaning given by section 12(1) above ;

" fodder " means hay or other substance commonly used for food of animals ;

" horse " includes ass and mule ;

" imported " means brought to Great Britain from a country out of Great Britain ;

" inspector " means a person appointed to be an inspector for the purposes of this Act by the Minister or by a local authority, and, when used in relation to an officer of the Ministry, includes a veterinary inspector ;

" justice " means justice of the peace ;

" litter " means straw or other substance commonly used for bedding or otherwise for or about animals ;

" local authority " has the meaning given by section 50 above ;

" order of the Minister " means an order under this Act of the Minister, the appropriate Minister, or the Ministers, as the case may be ;

" pleuro-pneumonia " means contagious pleuro-pneumonia of cattle ;

' pony " means any horse not more than 147 centimetres in height, except a foal travelling with its dam if the dam is over 147 centimetres ;

" suspected " means suspected of being diseased ;

" swine-fever " means the disease known as typhoid fever of swine, soldier purples, red disease, hog cholera or swine-plague ;

" veterinary inspector " means a veterinary inspector appointed by the Minister.

(2) In the computation of time for the purposes of this Act, a period reckoned by days from the happening of an event or the doing of an act or thing shall be deemed to be exclusive of the day on which the event happened or the act or thing is done.

90. The enactments and instruments with respect to which provision may be made by Order in Council in pursuance of section 1(1)(*h*) of the Hovercraft Act 1968 include this Act and any instrument made or having effect as if made under it.

This section is without prejudice to section 17 of the Interpretation Act 1978 (repeal and re-enactment).

PART VI
1978 c. 30.

91.—(1) The Minister, the appropriate Minister or the Ministers, as the case may be, shall publish in the London Gazette and the Edinburgh Gazette a notice of any order of the Minister stating—   Orders etc.

    (*a*) that the order has been made ; and

    (*b*) where copies of the order may be obtained.

(2) Every local authority shall at their own expense publish every order of the Minister, and every licence or other instrument sent to them by the Minister, the appropriate Minister, or the Ministers—

    (*a*) in such manner as he or they shall direct ; and

    (*b*) subject to and in the absence of any direction, by advertisement in a newspaper circulating in the district of the local authority.

(3) The validity or effect of an order of the Minister, or licence or other instrument issued by the Minister, the appropriate Minister or the Ministers shall not be affected by want of or defect or irregularity in its publication.

(4) Subsections (1) to (3) above do not apply to an order made under section 32 above.

(5) A power conferred by this Act to make an order of the Minister, other than by—

    (*a*) section 14(2),

    (*b*) section 59(1),

shall be exercisable by statutory instrument.

(6) An order of the Minister made under either of the provisions referred to in paragraphs (*a*) and (*b*) of subsection (5) above may be altered or revoked by a subsequent order made in the like manner and subject to the like conditions, but section 14(*b*) of the Interpretation Act 1978 shall not apply to an order made by the Ministers under section 34(7) above providing that section 34(6) shall cease to have effect.   1978 c. 30.

Scotland and Northern Ireland

92.—(1) The provisions of this section have effect for the purposes of the application of this Act to Scotland.   General application to Scotland.

(2) An offence against this Act may be prosecuted in the district court, and, when so prosecuted, the provisions in relation to sentences contained in section 284 of the Criminal Procedure (Scotland) Act 1975 shall apply to such a prosecution as they apply to prosecutions of common law offences.   1975 c. 21.

PART VI

(3) In the event of refusal or delay on the part of any person in complying with the order of a local authority, the local authority may give information of the refusal or delay to the procurator-fiscal of the district, who may apply to the sheriff for a warrant to carry such order into effect, and such warrant may be executed by the officers of the court in common form.

(4) Notwithstanding anything in any other Act, and except in relation to section 4 above, such part not exceeding one half of every fine recovered under this Act as the court before which it is recovered thinks fit shall be paid to the person who proceeds for it.

(5) Nothing in subsections (3) and (4) above applies to proceedings under the customs and excise Acts.

1935 c. 31.
1919 c. 91.

(6) Notwithstanding the repeal by this Act of section 17 of the Diseases of Animals Act 1935, Part I of the Ministry of Agriculture and Fisheries Act 1919 shall be deemed always to have extended to Scotland.

Communications to and from Northern Ireland.

93. In order to secure uniformity of action—

    (*a*) every order of the Minister shall with all practicable speed be communicated to the Department of Agriculture for Northern Ireland ; and

    (*b*) every order made by that Department under the enactments in Northern Ireland relating to diseases of animals shall with all practicable speed be communicated to the Minister.

Miscellaneous provisions as to operation

Transitional.

94.—(1) Where a period of time specified in an enactment repealed by this Act is current at the commencement of this Act, this Act shall have effect as if the corresponding provisions of this Act had been in force when that period began to run.

(2) For the purpose of determining the punishment which may be imposed on a person in respect of the commission by him of an offence under any provision of this Act, an offence committed by that person under the corresponding enactment repealed by this Act shall be deemed to have been committed under that provision.

Savings.
1950 c. 36.

95.—(1) Any order made or having effect as if made—

    (*a*) under any provision of sections 24 to 33 of the Diseases of Animals Act 1950,

1975 c. 40.

    (*b*) before the coming into operation of section 1 of the Diseases of Animals Act 1975, continues in operation as if that section had not come into operation, except that it may be varied or revoked as if it had been made under section 10 above.

(2) In the case of an order made or having effect as if made—

    (a) partly under any provision of those sections of that Act of 1950, and

    (b) partly under any other enactment (whether or not contained in that Act),

subsection (1) above has effect to the extent that the order was made or had effect as if made under any of those sections.

(3) The Conveyance of Live Poultry Order 1919, made under the Poultry Act 1911, has effect as if it had been made under sections 7(2), 37(1) and 64(2) above. S.R. & O. 1919/933. 1911 c. 11.

(4) Without prejudice to section 17 of the Interpretation Act 1978 (repeal and re-enactment), the power conferred by virtue of sections 135(2) and 136(3) of the Medicines Act 1968 to bring into operation Schedule 6 to that Act (enactments of Parliament of United Kingdom repealed) has effect as if that Schedule included references to section 5(2) above and Schedule 1 to this Act. 1978 c. 30. 1968 c. 67.

(5) Any officer or servant employed by the Minister for the purpose of the execution of the enactments relating to diseases of animals who was appointed before the commencement of Part IV of the Agriculture Act 1937 (1st April 1938) shall be deemed to have been appointed under section 5 of the Board of Agriculture Act 1889. 1937 c. 70. 1889 c. 30.

(6) Nothing in this Act affects sections 40(2) and 42(2) of the Northern Ireland Constitution Act 1973 as those subsections have effect in relation to section 88 of the Diseases of Animals Act 1950. 1973 c. 36. 1950 c. 36.

(7) In so far as any provision of—

    (a) paragraph (a) of section 35(4) above,

    (b) paragraph (a)(ii) of section 41(1) above,

    (c) paragraph (c) of section 75(1) above, and

    (d) section 89(1) above,

specifies an amount expressed in metric units which is derived from the exercise of the power to make regulations under section 7 of the Agriculture (Miscellaneous Provisions) Act 1976 that provision may be varied as if it were contained in regulations so made. 1976 c. 55.

96.—(1) The enactments specified in Schedule 5 to this Act have effect subject to the amendments specified in that Schedule being amendments consequential on the provisions of this Act. Consequential amendments and repeals.

PART VI

(2) The enactments specified in Schedule 6 to this Act (which include certain obsolete or unnecessary enactments) are repealed to the extent specified in the third column of that Schedule.

Short title, extent, and commencement.

1950 c. 36.

97.—(1) This Act may be cited as the Animal Health Act 1981.

(2) Sections 93 and 95(6) above apply to Northern Ireland, and Schedule 6 to this Act, so far as it repeals provisions of the Diseases of Animals Act 1950 which applied to Northern Ireland, but apart from those provisions this Act does not extend to Northern Ireland.

(3) This Act shall come into force on the expiry of the period of one month beginning on the date of its passing.

SCHEDULES

SCHEDULE 1

REGULATION OF MANUFACTURE OF AND OTHER MATTERS CONNECTED WITH VETERINARY THERAPEUTIC SUBSTANCES

Substances to which this Schedule applies

1.—(1) Subject to the provisions of sub-paragraph (2) below, this Schedule applies—

(*a*) to the therapeutic substances specified in paragraph 5 below ; and

(*b*) to any other therapeutic substances capable of being used for veterinary purposes which may from time to time be added to that paragraph as being substances the purity or potency of which cannot be adequately tested by chemical means.

(2) In the case of any substance mentioned in sub-paragraph (1) above which is a substance to which the Therapeutic Substances Act 1956 c. 25. 1956 applies, this Schedule applies to that substance in so far only as the substance is excluded from the operation of that Act, as being intended to be used solely for veterinary purposes, by regulations made under that Act.

Power to make orders as to substances to which this Schedule applies

2.—(1) The Ministers may make orders for the following purposes—

(*a*) for adding to paragraph 5 below any therapeutic substance capable of being used for veterinary purposes, the purity or potency of which cannot be adequately tested by chemical means ;

(*b*) for prohibiting, except under a licence for the purpose issued by the appropriate Minister and in accordance with any conditions subject to which the licence is issued, the manufacture for sale or the importation into Great Britain of any such substance to which this Schedule applies as may be specified in the order ;

(*c*) for prescribing the standard of strength, quality and purity of any substance in respect of which an order made for the purpose last mentioned is in force ;

(*d*) for prescribing the tests to be used for determining whether the standard prescribed as mentioned above has been attained ;

(*e*) for prescribing units of standardisation ;

(*f*) for prescribing the form of licences and of applications for them, and of notices to be given in connection with them ;

(*g*) for prescribing the conditions subject to which licences may be issued, including, in the case of a licence to manufacture conditions that the manufacture shall be carried on only upon the premises specified in the licence and that the licensee shall allow any inspector authorised by the Minister in that behalf to enter any premises where the manufacture is carried on, and to inspect the premises and plant and the process of manufacture and the means employed for standardising and testing the manufactured substance and to take samples of it ;

(*h*) for prescribing any other matter which under this Schedule is to be prescribed.

(2) The Ministers may make orders as respects any such substance to which this Schedule applies as may be specified in the order—

(*a*) requiring that, if advertised or sold as a proprietary medicine or contained in such medicine, such accepted scientific name or name descriptive of the true nature or origin of the substance as may be prescribed shall appear on the label ;

(*b*) requiring that the date of the manufacture shall be stated in the prescribed manner on all vessels or other packages in which the substance is sold or offered for sale, and prohibiting the sale of the substance after the expiry of the prescribed period from the date of manufacture ;

(*c*) prohibiting the sale or the offering for sale or the importation of the substance otherwise than in a vessel or other container of such character as may be prescribed, and requiring that the prescribed label or other description shall be affixed to such vessel or container.

Licences to manufacture

3.—(1) The following provisions shall have effect with respect to licences to manufacture for sale a substance the manufacture of which otherwise than under a licence is prohibited by an order—

(*a*) the licence shall be issued subject to such conditions as may be prescribed, may extend to all such substances or to such one or more of them as may be specified in the licence, shall continue in force for such period as may be prescribed, but may from time to time be renewed for a like period ;

(*b*) an applicant for a licence or the renewal of a licence must satisfy the appropriate Minister that the conditions under which the substance is to be manufactured by him and the premises in which it is to be manufactured are such as to comply with any order in force for the purposes of paragraph 2 above, and an applicant who so satisfies the appropriate Minister shall be entitled to the grant or renewal of the licence ;

(*c*) the appropriate Minister may revoke a licence or suspend it for such period as he thinks fit, if in his opinion the licensee has failed to comply with the conditions subject to which the licence was issued or with any such order as is mentioned above as to the prescribed standards of strength, quality and purity, and such revocation or suspension may apply to all the substances to which the licence extends or to some one or more of them.

(2) A person who is aggrieved by the revocation or suspension of his licence may, subject to rules of court, appeal to the court, whose decision shall be final.

(3) Nothing in any order prohibiting or regulating the manufacture for sale of any substance to which this Schedule applies shall apply to the preparation by a registered veterinary surgeon or practitioner—

    (*a*) for the treatment of any animal under his care, or

    (*b*) for and at the request of another such surgeon or practitioner,

of any such substance, if it is specially prepared with reference to the condition and for the treatment of an individual animal or bird.

(4) In this paragraph—

    " the court " means, as respects England and Wales, the High Court and, as respects Scotland, the Court of Session, and

    " registered " means, in relation to a veterinary surgeon, registered in pursuance of the Veterinary Surgeons Act 1966 in the register of veterinary surgeons and, in relation to a veterinary practitioner registered in pursuance of that Act in the Supplementary Veterinary Register.

    1966 c. 36.

Licences to import

4. The issue of a licence to import a substance the importation of which otherwise than under a licence is prohibited by an order shall be subject to such conditions, including conditions as to the strength, quality and purity of the substance and as to the suspension or revocation of the licence, as may be prescribed.

Therapeutic substances to which this Schedule applies

5. The therapeutic substances mentioned in paragraph 1(1)(*a*) above are—

    (1) The substances commonly known as vaccines, sera, toxins, antitoxins and antigens.

    (2) The substance commonly known as salvarsan (Dioxy-diamino-arseno-benzol-di-hydrochloride), and analogous substances used for the specific treatment of infective disease.

    (3) Extract of the pituitary body.

Offences under this Schedule

6. A person who—

    (*a*) contravenes or fails to comply with any condition subject to which any such licence as is mentioned in this Schedule is issued,

    (*b*) sells or offers for sale or has in his possession for sale any substance to which this Schedule applies knowing it to have been manufactured or imported in contravention of an order in force for any of the purposes of paragraph 2 above,

SCH. 2

(c) contravenes or fails to comply with the provisions of any such order as is mentioned above,

is liable on summary conviction to a fine not exceeding £50 or, in the case of a second or subsequent conviction, to such a fine or to imprisonment for a term not exceeding 2 months, and in either case to forfeit any goods in connection with which the offence was committed, and without prejudice, if the offender is the holder of a licence, to the power of the appropriate Minister to revoke or suspend the licence.

Section 10.

SCHEDULE 2

SPECIFIC MATTERS WITH RESPECT TO WHICH PROVISION MAY BE MADE IN ORDERS UNDER SECTION 10

1. The conditions to be observed before, during and after importation.

2. Exemptions from provisions of the order by means of licences, whether general or specific and whether conditional or unconditional, issued in accordance with the order.

3. The prohibition of the importation of animals or other things save at such ports, aerodromes and other places of entry as may be designated.

4. Landing and quarantine of animals and other things.

5. Seizure, detention and treatment of animals and other things.

6. Slaughter of animals and destruction of other things.

7. Cleansing and disinfection.

8. Marking, testing and use of animals and other things.

9. Movement of persons and of animals and other things.

10. Recovery of costs.

11. Inspection.

12. Entitlement to compensation and the determination, subject to the Treasury's approval, of the amount of compensation payable in any case.

Section 31.

SCHEDULE 3

POWER TO SLAUGHTER IN RELATION TO CERTAIN DISEASES

Cattle plague

1.—(1) The Minister shall cause to be slaughtered all animals affected with cattle plague.

(2) Where an animal is or has been in the same shed, stable, herd or flock as, or in contact with, an animal affected with cattle plague, the Minister may, if he is satisfied that the slaughter of the animal is necessary for preventing the spreading of cattle plague, cause the animal to be slaughtered.

(3) The Minister may, if he thinks fit, in any case cause to be slaughtered—

> (*a*) any animals suspected of being affected with cattle plague, or being in a place infected with cattle plague ;
>
> (*b*) any animals being in such parts of an area infected with cattle plague as are not comprised in a place infected with cattle plague (but in this last-mentioned case subject to such regulations as the Treasury by statutory instrument think fit to make).

(4) The Minister shall for animals slaughtered under this paragraph pay compensation as follows—

> (*a*) where the animal slaughtered was affected with cattle plague, the compensation shall be one half of its value immediately before it became so affected, but so that the compensation does not in any such case exceed £20 ; and
>
> (*b*) in every other case the compensation shall be the value of the animal immediately before it was slaughtered, but so that the compensation does not in any case exceed £40.

Pleuro-pneumonia

2.—(1) The Minister shall cause to be slaughtered all cattle affected with pleuro-pneumonia.

(2) The Minister may, if he thinks fit, in any case cause to be slaughtered—

> (*a*) any cattle suspected of being affected with pleuro-pneumonia ; and
>
> (*b*) any cattle which are or which have been in the same field, shed, or other place, or in the same herd or otherwise in contact with cattle affected with pleuro-pneumonia, or which appear to the Minister to have been in any way exposed to the infection of pleuro-pneumonia.

(3) The Minister shall for cattle slaughtered under this paragraph pay compensation as follows—

> (*a*) where the animal slaughtered was affected with pleuro-pneumonia, the compensation shall be three-fourths of the value of the animal immediately before it became so affected, but so that the compensation does not in any such case exceed £30 ; and
>
> (*b*) in every other case the compensation shall be the value of the animal immediately before it was slaughtered, but so that the compensation does not in any case exceed £40.

(4) Where the Minister has decided that any head of cattle is to be slaughtered under this paragraph, the Minister shall, if the owner of such head of cattle by notice in writing so requires cause the same to be slaughtered within 21 days after the receipt of the notice.

Foot-and-mouth disease

3.—(1) The Minister may, if he thinks fit, in any case cause to be slaughtered—

   (a) any animals affected with foot-and-mouth disease, or suspected of being so affected ; and

   (b) any animals which are or have been in the same field, shed, or other place, or in the same herd or flock, or otherwise in contact with animals affected with foot-and-mouth disease, or which appear to the Minister to have been in any way exposed to the infection of foot-and-mouth disease.

(2) The Minister shall for animals slaughtered under this paragraph pay compensation as follows—

   (a) where the animal slaughtered was affected with foot-and-mouth disease the compensation shall be the value of the animal immediately before it became so affected ;

   (b) in every other case the compensation shall be the value of the animal immediately before it was slaughtered.

Swine-fever

4.—(1) The Minister may, if he thinks fit, in any case cause to be slaughtered—

   (a) any swine affected with swine-fever, or suspected of being so affected ; and

   (b) any swine which are or have been in the same field, pig-sty, shed, or other place, or in the same herd, or otherwise in contact with swine affected with swine-fever, or which appear to the Minister to have been in any way exposed to the infection of swine-fever.

(2) The Minister shall for animals slaughtered under this paragraph pay compensation as follows—

   (a) where the animal slaughtered was affected with swine-fever, the compensation shall be one half of the value of the animal immediately before it became so affected ;

   (b) in every other case the compensation shall be the value of the animal immediately before it was slaughtered.

Diseases of poultry

5.—(1) The Minister may, if he thinks fit, cause to be slaughtered—

   (a) any diseased or suspected poultry ; or

   (b) any poultry which are or have been in the same field, pen, shed or other place as, or otherwise in contact with, diseased poultry or which appear to the Minister to have been in any way exposed to the infection of disease.

(2) The Minister shall for poultry, other than diseased poultry, slaughtered under this paragraph pay compensation, which shall be the value of the bird immediately before it was slaughtered.

(3) The Minister may by order prescribe the payment of compensation in accordance with a scale approved by the Treasury for

diseased poultry slaughtered under this paragraph, being poultry
affected with any disease other than fowl pest in any of its forms,
including Newcastle disease and fowl plague.

SCH. 3

SCHEDULE 4

Section 38(2).

ADDITIONAL PROVISIONS AS TO FOOD AND WATER AT RAILWAY STATIONS

1. The food and water, or either of them, provided under section
38(2) above shall be supplied to the animal by the body carrying
the animal on the request—

(*a*) of the consignor ; or

(*b*) of any person in charge of the animal.

2. As regards water, if, in the case of any animal, such a request
is not made, so that the animal remains without a supply of water
for 24 consecutive hours—

(*a*) the consignor and the person in charge of the animal shall
each be guilty of an offence against this Act ; and

(*b*) it shall lie on the person charged to prove such a request
and the time within which the animal had a supply of
water.

3. The Ministers may, if they think fit, by order prescribe any
other period, not less than 12 hours instead of the period of 24
hours mentioned above, either generally, or in respect of any particular kind of animals.

4. The body supplying food or water under section 38(2) may
make in respect of that supply such reasonable charges (if any)
as the Ministers by order approve, in addition to such charges as
they are for the time being authorised to make in respect of the
carriage of animals.

5. The amount of those additional charges accrued due in respect
of any animal shall be a debt from the consignor and from the
consignee of the animal to the body concerned, and shall be recoverable by the body concerned, with costs, by proceedings in any court
of competent jurisdiction.

6. The body concerned shall have a lien for the amount of that
debt on the animal in respect of which the debt accrued due, and
on any other animal at any time consigned by or to the same
consignor or consignee to be carried by that body.

SCHEDULE 5

Section 96

CONSEQUENTIAL AMENDMENTS

Protection of Birds Act 1954

1. In paragraph (*b*) of section 4(1) of the Protection of Birds Act
1954 for " Minister of Agriculture and Fisheries by or under the
Diseases of Animals Act, 1950 " substitute " Minister of Agriculture, Fisheries and Food, or on the Secretary of State, or on the

1954 c. **30.**

SCH. 5   Minister and the Secretary of State acting jointly, by or under the Animal Health Act 1981 ".

1955 c. 16
(4 & 5 Eliz. 2).

Food and Drugs Act 1955

2. In section 100(6) of the Food and Drugs Act 1955 for " Diseases of Animals Act 1950 " substitute " Animal Health Act 1981 ".

1956 c. 30.

Food and Drugs (Scotland) Act 1956

3. In section 36(6) of the Food and Drugs (Scotland) Act 1956 for " Diseases of Animals Act 1950 " substitute " Animal Health Act 1981 ".

1963 c. 11.

Agriculture (Miscellaneous Provisions) Act 1963

4. In section 16(3) of the Agriculture (Miscellaneous Provisions) Act 1963 for " either of the preceding subsections " substitute " the preceding subsection ", and omit the words—

    (a) " the Minister to whom the fee was paid or, as the case may be," ; and

    (b) " he or ".

1963 c. 33.

London Government Act 1963

5. In section 54(3) of the London Government Act 1963 for " Diseases of Animals Act 1950 " substitute " Animal Health Act 1981 ".

1963 c. 43.

Animal Boarding Establishments Act 1963

6. In paragraph (b) of the proviso to section 5(1) of the Animal Boarding Establishments Act 1963 for " Diseases of Animals Act 1950 " substitute " Animal Health Act 1981 ".

1967 c. 22.

Agriculture Act 1967

7. In section 13(5) of the Agriculture Act 1967 for " Diseases of Animals Act 1950 " substitute " Animal Health Act 1981 ".

1968 c. 34.

Agriculture (Miscellaneous Provisions) Act 1968

8. In section 8(2) of the Agriculture (Miscellaneous Provisions) Act 1968—

    (a) for " section 59 of the Diseases of Animals Act 1950 " substitute " section 50 of the Animal Health Act 1981 " ; and

    (b) for " in subsection (2) the words from ' and shall ' onwards were omitted " substitute " paragraph (b)(ii) were omitted from subsection (2) ".

Transport Act 1968

SCH. 5
1968 c. 73.

9. In paragraph 7(2)(*b*) of Schedule 16 to the Transport Act 1968 for " section 22 of the Diseases of Animals Act 1950 " substitute " section 38(2) of and Schedule 4 to the Animal Health Act 1981 ".

Agriculture Act 1970

1970 c. 40.

10. In section 106(6) of the Agriculture Act 1970 for " Diseases of Animals Act 1950 " substitute " Animal Health Act 1981 ".

Slaughterhouses Act 1974

1974 c. 3.

11. In the Slaughterhouses Act 1974—

(*a*) in section 20(5) for " Diseases of Animals Act 1950 " substitute " Animal Health Act 1981 " ;

(*b*) in section 35 for " Diseases of Animals Act 1950 " substitute " Animal Health Act 1981 " ;

(*c*) in paragraph (*b*) of section 38(2), and in section 39(2), for " Diseases of Animals Act 1950 " substitute " Animal Health Act 1981 " ;

(*d*) in paragraph (*d*) of section 40(3) for " section 20 of the Diseases of Animals Act 1950 " substitute " paragraphs (*a*) and (*b*) of section 7(1), paragraphs (*b*) to (*e*) of section 8(1), section 25 and section 37(1) of the Animal Health Act 1981 " ;

(*e*) in section 42(3) for " Diseases of Animals Act 1950 " substitute " Animal Health Act 1981 ".

Slaughter of Animals (Scotland) Act 1980

1980 c. 13.

12. In the Slaughter of Animals (Scotland) Act 1980—

(*a*) in section 13(4) and 15(1) for " Diseases of Animals Act 1950 " substitute " Animal Health Act 1981 " ;

(*b*) in paragraph (*e*) of section 16(4) for " section 20 of the Diseases of Animals Act 1950 " substitute " paragraphs (*a*) and (*b*) of section 7(1), paragraphs (*b*) to (*e*) of section 8(1), section 25 and section 37(1) of the Animal Health Act 1981 ".

SCHEDULE 6

REPEALS

Chapter	Short title	Extent of repeal
25 & 26 Geo. 5. c. 31.	Diseases of Animals Act 1935.	The whole Act.
14 Geo. 6. c. 36.	Diseases of Animals Act 1950.	The whole Act.
2 & 3 Eliz. 2. c. 39.	Agriculture (Miscellaneous Provisions) Act 1954.	Section 11. Schedule 2.
4 & 5 Eliz. 2. c. 46.	Administration of Justice Act 1956.	Section 49(2).
10 & 11 Eliz. 2. c. 46.	Transport Act 1962.	In Part I of Schedule 2, the entry relating to the Diseases of Animals Act 1950.
1963 c. 11.	Agriculture (Miscellaneous Provisions) Act 1963.	Sections 13 and 14. Section 16(1). In section 16(3), the words— (a) " the Minister to whom the fee was paid or, as the case may be,"; and (b) " he or ".
1963 c. 33.	London Government Act 1963.	In section 54(4), the words " The Diseases of Animals Act 1950 ". In Part I of Schedule 13, paragraph 1.
1967 c. 22.	Agriculture Act 1967.	Section 66.
1967 c. 80.	Criminal Justice Act 1967.	In Part I of Schedule 3, the entry relating to the Diseases of Animals Act 1950.
1968 c. 67.	Medicines Act 1968.	In Schedule 6, the entry relating to Part II of and Schedule 3 to the Diseases of Animals Act 1950.
1969 c. 28.	Ponies Act 1969.	The whole Act.
1970 c. 40.	Agriculture Act 1970.	Section 105(2) to (5). Section 106(3).
1971 c. 23.	Courts Act 1971.	In Part I of Schedule 9, the entry relating to the Diseases of Animals Act 1950.
1972 c. 62.	Agriculture (Miscellaneous Provisions) Act 1972.	Sections 1 to 3.
1972 c. 68.	European Communities Act 1972.	In Schedule 4, paragraph 7.
1973 c. 65.	Local Government (Scotland) Act 1973.	Section 144(1), (2).
1974 c. 7.	Local Government Act 1974.	In Schedule 6, paragraph 7.
1974 c. 17.	Rabies Act 1974.	The whole Act.
1975 c. 40.	Diseases of Animals Act 1975.	The whole Act.

Chapter	Short title	Extent of repeal
1976 c. 55.	Agriculture (Miscellaneous Provisions) Act 1976.	Sections 8 to 10. In Schedule 3, the reference to the Diseases of Animals Act 1950.
1976 c. 63.	Bail Act 1976.	In Schedule 2, paragraph 13.
1977 c. 45.	Criminal Law Act 1977.	Section 55(1) to (3).
1979 c. 2.	Customs and Excise Management Act 1979.	In Part I of the Table of textual amendments in paragraph 12 of Schedule 4, the entry relating to the Diseases of Animals Act 1950.

PRINTED IN ENGLAND BY W. J. SHARP
Controller and Chief Executive of Her Majesty's Stationery Office and
Queen's Printer of Acts of Parliament